The Language of Advertising

TORBEN VESTERGAARD
and
KIM SCHRØDER

Basil Blackwell

© Torben Vestergaard and Kim Schrøder 1985

First published 1985

Basil Blackwell Publisher Ltd
108 Cowley Road, Oxford OX4 1JF, UK

Basil Blackwell Inc.
432 Park Avenue South, Suite 1505,
New York, NY 10016, USA

British Library Cataloguing in Publication Data

Vestergaard, Torben
   The Language of Advertising—(Language
in society; 9)
   1. Advertising—Psychological aspects
   2. Advertising—Social aspects
   I. Title   II. Series
   302.2′3   HF5822

   ISBN 0-631-10741-X
   ISBN 0-631-12743-7 Pbk

Library of Congress Cataloging in Publication Data

Vestergaard, Torben, 1943-
   The Language of Advertising

(Language in society; 9)
   Bibliography: p. 178
   Includes index.
   1. Advertising—Language.   I. Schrøder, Kim.
   II. Title.   II. Series: Language in society (Oxford,
   Oxfordshire); 9.
   HF5827.V47 1985   659.1′014   84-14455

   ISBN 0-631-10741-X
   ISBN 0-631-12743-7 (pbk.)

Typeset by System 4 Associates, Gerrards Cross, Bucks
Printed in Great Britain by T. J. Press Ltd, Padstow, Cornwall

Contents

List of Plates   v
Editor's Preface   vii
Acknowledgements   ix

1 Advertising and Society   1
   What is advertising?   1
   Is advertising necessary?   3
   The function of advertising   7
   The scope of this book   9

2 Language and Communication   13
   The verbal message   14
   The visual message   32

3 The Structure of an Advertisement   49
   The adman's task   49
   Two examples   50
   Attention and interest   58
   Desire and conviction   65
   Action   67

4 Strategies of Address: Sex and Class   71
   Audience targeting   71
   Men and women   73
   Addressing women   79
   Addressing men   102
   Addessing men and women: conclusion   108
   Addressing the classes   110

5 Advertising as a Psychological Mirror   117
   Introduction   117
   Taking the ideological temperature   120
   The Utopia of youth and leisure   122
   Advertisements as a socio-psychological diagnosis   124
   Conclusion   139

6 The Ideology of Advertising   141
   Introduction   141
   Ideology   145
   Specific ideologies of advertising   152
   'Recuperative' advertising   163
   Reforming advertising?   168

   Notes   175

   Bibliography   178

   Index   181

List of Plates

1	'Howdy!'	33
2	Stella Artois	37
3	Red Silk Cut	40
4	Car company symbols	41
5	Avon	45
6	The Kings and Queens Collection	47
7	Dr White's	51
8	Scottish Widows	55
9	Babette	59
10	Cutex	63
11	Schloer	64
12	Simplicity	72
13	Close-up	76
14	Close-up	77
15	Tao	83
16	Anne French	85
17	Max Factor	86
18	Tampax	91
19	British Gas	92
20	Soft & Gentle	95
21	Vichy Skin Care	98
22	Sally Hansen	99
23	Max Factor	101
24	English Leather Musk	105
25	Rothmans	107
26	Lancôme	109
27	Pyrex	114
28	Estivalia	119

29	Singles Society	125
30	Abbey National	128
31	Pears	130
32	Farmhouse Cheese	134
33	MG	136
34	Ravel Shoes	137
35	Vu	138
36	Londun Line	144
37	Whitbread	151
38	Tampax	161
39	Cabriole	166
40	Smirnoff	169
41	Johnson's Baby Shampoo	171
42	Hoover	173

Editor's Preface

Advertising is something that we are all exposed to. It is also something that is likely to affect most of us in a number of different spheres of our lives. Advertising takes many forms, but in most of them language is of crucial importance. The wording of advertisements is, in most cases, carefully crafted to meet particular ends. Sometimes it is intended to inform, but more often, and more importantly, to persuade and influence. Advertising, moreover, not only influences any human society in which it is widespread but also reflects certain aspects of that society's values and that society's structure. The *Language in Society* series is therefore an ideal location for the publication of the present volume. The book is a pioneering and excellent example of that sort of applied sociolinguistics which can perhaps be best described as the study of language use. More often than not, linguists are concerned to investigate the properties of language as such — language as a code. The authors of this book, though, have turned their analytical ability and linguistic expertise to an examination not only of the linguistic forms used in advertising but also of their content. They are, it is true, interested in the linguistic characteristics of the language of advertisements, but they are also vitally concerned with what advertisements do and (crucially) don't say. Since they are also clearly interested in the societal impetuses that lie behind particular types of advertising, and in advertising's social repercussions, we can say that this book is truly an investigation into the role of language in society.

Peter Trudgill

Acknowledgements

The authors and publishers would like to thank the following, who gave permission for their advertisements to be reproduced in this book: A. & F. Pears Limited (plate 31); Abbey National Building Society (plate 30); Antonio Puig S.A. and Agencia de Publicidad de Servicios Generales (plate 28); Associated Press (plate 1); Austin Rover Group Limited (plate 33); Avon Overseas Ltd (plate 5); Babette Exports Limited (plate 9); Beecham Group plc (plate 8); British Gas Corporation (plate 19); Carreras Rothmans Limited (plate 25); Chaussures Ravel Limited (plate 34); Chesebrough-Ponds Ltd (plate 10); Colgate-Palmolive Limited (plate 20); Corning Limited (plate 27); Dairy Crest (plate 32); Dateline International (plate 29); Elida Gibbs Limited (plates 13 and 14); Elizabeth Arden Limited (plate 39); Gallaher Limited (plate 3); Hoover plc (plate 42); International Chemical Company Limited (plate 16); International Distillers and Vintners (UK) Limited (plate 40); Johnson & Johnson Limited (plate 41); Kimberly-Clark Limited (plate 12); Lilia-White Limited (plate 7); Max Factor & Co (UK) Ltd (plates 17 and 23); Mem Company, Inc. (plate 24); Parim Limited (plates 26 and 35); Royal Society of British Sculptors and The Franklin Mint (plate 6); Sally Hansen Ltd (plate 22); Scottish Widows' Fund and Life Assurance Society (plate 8); Tampax Limited (plates 18 and 38); The Tao Clinic (plate 15); Twins Products (Pty) Ltd (plate 36); Vichy (UK) Limited (plate 21); Whitbread & Company, plc (plates 2 and 37).

The following kindly gave permission for the use of quotations from advertisements for their products or services: Ashe Laboratories Ltd (Amplex); Beecham Proprietaries (Yeastvite); Birds Eye Wall's Limited (Birds Eye); Brook Bond Oxo Ltd (Oxo); Crosby

Kitchens Limited; Eylure Ltd (Easiface); Fisons plc (Sanatogen); Imperial Tobacco Limited; John A. Frye Shoe Company, Inc. (Frye Boots); Langham Life Assurance Company Limited; Larkhall Laboratories (Aquamaid); Lyle & Scott Ltd (Jockey); Max Factor & Co. (UK) Ltd (Miners and Rapport); Mem Company, Inc. (Racquet Club); The Mentholatum Company Limited (Stop 'n Grow); Nairn Floors Limited; Nicholas Laboratories Limited (Radox); Rimmel International Limited; R. J. Reynolds Tobacco International (Camel); Schwarzkopf Limited; Valvoline Oil Company; Van den Berghs (Flora); Volvo Car Corporation; Yardley of London Limited (Chique).

We would like to thank the following persons and institutions. Colleagues who have read and commented on the manuscript at various stages especially Mr Ulf Hedetoft, Mrs Shirley Larsen, Ms Signe Eskelund, Mr Frede Østergaard; students of ours who found quite a few of the advertisements used in the book; Ms Signe Frits and Ms Bente Kragh, who have typed the manuscript; finally the editor of the series, Professor Peter Trudgill, and the staff of Basil Blackwell for their advice and, not least, their patience.

Torben Vestergaard
Kim Schrøder

1

Advertising and Society

WHAT IS ADVERTISING?

At first sight this question might seem a bit superfluous. After all, advertising is with us all the time: whenever we open a newspaper or a magazine, turn on the TV, or look at the hoardings in tube stations or on buildings, we are confronted with advertisements. Most of these will be of the type which Leech (1966: 25) describes as 'commercial consumer advertising'. This is indeed the most frequent type, the type on which most money and skill is spent, and the type which affects us most deeply, but there are others.

In the first place it is possible to distinguish between non-commercial and commercial advertising. As examples of non-commercial advertising one may mention communication from government agencies to citizens like the British metrication campaign, or appeals from various associations and societies, whether their purposes are charity or political propaganda.

Commercial advertising covers first the so-called prestige or good-will advertising, where firms advertise not a commodity or a service, but rather a name or an image. This type of advertising aims at creating long-term goodwill with the public rather than at an immediate increase in sales. Examples are particularly frequent in the business pages of the Sunday papers where large firms often publish extracts of their reports and accounts. Since shareholders will receive this information by post anyway, the only purpose of these advertisements must be to remind people of the existence of the firm and to leave a generally favourable impression. In some cases prestige advertising contains a more or less explicit element of political propaganda. Consider the following extract from a two-page advertisement for Exxon (in Europe: Esso) which appeared in the American *Ms Magazine* in September 1976:

> Who's really qualified to tackle America's energy needs?
> Experienced companies who can take the technology they've developed in one area and make it work in another.
> Exxon has been doing it — for years.

In addition to boosting the prestige of the particular firm behind the advert, this advert is intended to make the public adopt the same attitude as the industry towards what is regarded as undue government interference.

The second type of commercial advertising is known as industrial or trade advertising. Here a firm advertises its products or services to other firms. Industrial advertising is most likely to be found in specialized trade journals or, again, in the business pages of newspapers. This type of advertising differs from both prestige advertising and consumer advertising in that it can be regarded as communication between equals (see pp. 7-8), that is, both the advertiser and the prospective reader have a special interest in and a particular knowledge about the product or service advertised. For this reason industrial advertising typically lays greater emphasis on factual information than prestige and consumer advertising, and, inversely, less emphasis on the persuasive elements.

Harris and Seldon (1962: 40) define advertising as a public notice 'designed to spread information with a view to promoting the sales of marketable goods and services'. This definition will be seen to cover both industrial advertising and commercial consumer advertising, where the advertiser is a firm appealing to individual private consumers rather than to other firms. The two participants in the communication situation (see further chapter 2) defined by consumer advertising are thus *un*equal as far as interest in and knowledge about the product advertised are concerned (cf. Wight 1972: 9, 'amateur buyers facing a professional seller'), and the central concern of this book will be to investigate how the use of language is affected by the function it has to serve in this particular situation. For this reason — and because it *is* the most important type — we shall deal almost exclusively with consumer advertising; some comments will be made on prestige advertising, but industrial advertising will not be dealt with.

Yet another distinction can be made between classified and display advertising. In newspapers and magazines, display advertisements are placed in prominent places amongst the editorial material in order to attract the attention of readers whose main interest in the publication is not this or that particular advert. Classified advertisements, on the other hand, are placed on special pages and ordered (classified) according to subject. Normally, classified adverts will be read only by readers with a special interest in some particular product or service. Moreover, the display advertisement is typically inserted by a large firm or association — normally through the mediation of a professional advertising agency — whereas the advertiser behind a classified advert is normally a smaller local firm or private individual who will have drafted it himself. Classified advertising thus lacks two of the characteristics of other advertising. First, although classified adverts are of course inserted 'with a view to promoting the sales', persuasive elements are often virtually absent and, at any rate, nothing or very little is done to persuade prospective buyers to *read* the advert. A classified advert thus comes very close to being merely a notice informing interested segments of the public that something is available at a certain price. Second, because of the shared interest in the thing advertised, classified advertising is also quite close to being communication between equals. This is, of course, most clearly the case when the advertiser is a private individual, in which case the product cannot even be considered a commodity (for the distinction between product and commodity, see p. 8).

IS ADVERTISING NECESSARY?

But why is there such a thing as advertising, and why does it have to be persuasive? Why cannot advertisers merely inform consumers of the availability and price of a commodity and leave them to decide for themselves whether to buy or not? The answer to both questions is to be found in the social conditions which make advertising possible and in which our consumption takes place.

As long as the productive apparatus of a society is not sufficiently developed to satisfy more than the barest material needs of its population, there is of course no scope for advertising. For advertising to make sense at all, at least a segment of the population must live above subsistence level; and the very moment this situation occurs it also becomes necessary for the producers of materially 'unnecessary' goods to do something to make people want to acquire their commodities. However, advertising is not just any sales-promoting activity — door-to-door salesmanship is not, for instance, and this points to the second precondition for advertising: the existence of a (relatively) mass market and media through which it can be reached. In Britain the emergence of a relatively large, literate middle class in the early eighteenth century created the preconditions for advertising in its modern sense. Advertisements from that period were directed at frequenters of coffee houses, where magazines and newspapers were read (Turner 1965: 23), and, significantly, the products advertised were such 'luxuries' as coffee, tea, books, wigs, patent medicines, cosmetics, plays and concerts, and lottery tickets.

However, the great breakthrough for advertising only came in the late nineteenth century. Technology and mass-production techniques were now sufficiently developed for more firms to be able to turn out products of roughly the same quality and at roughly the same price. This was accompanied by overproduction and underdemand (Turner 1965: 132-4) which meant that the market had to be stimulated, so advertising technique changed from proclamation to persuasion. At the same time literacy had spread to ever larger segments of the population, and the first newspaper to rely on advertising for a significant part of its revenue, the *Daily Mail*, began publication in this period (in 1896; see *British Press* 1976: 3). Finally, the late nineteenth century was the period in which advertising became a profession of its own with the establishment of the first advertising agencies.

The social and institutional setting in which advertising exists today has thus been present since the beginning of this century: mass-produced goods, a mass market reached through mass publications whose single most important source of revenue is advertising,[1] and a professional advertising trade handling all major advertising accounts.

The most important new development in this century is without any doubt the advent of a new advertising medium, television, co-inciding — in Europe — with the post-war economic boom which began in the 1950s. These two factors triggered off, and may in turn have been accelerated by, an increase in advertising activity: advertising expenditure in Britain rose from 0.9 per cent of gross national product in 1952 to 1.4 per cent in 1960, or from 1.2 to 1.9 per cent of total consumers' expenditure (Reekie 1974: 7-8). Reekie (ibid.) points out that this collection of circumstances may well have been one of the causes behind the increasing public interest in and disapproval of the methods of advertising in the late fifties and early sixties. Consumerists such as Packard (1957) called for more truthful, that is to say more informative and less persuasive, advertising, while apologists of advertising answered that advertising was frankly and legitimately persuasive, but that it persuaded by being informative (Harris and Seldon 1962: 74). Let us look at the conception underlying the consumerists' demand for less persuasive and more informative advertising. This will provide the answer to the second 'why' asked at the beginning of this section.

In its extreme form the consumerist position seems to rest on an incomplete understanding of the needs which people satisfy through the consumption of goods. We all need food and drink enough to keep us alive, clothes to keep us warm and dry, and, under most climatic conditions, shelter against the weather; except under the most favourable conditions people may also need some means of transport to get from their dwelling to their sources of good. These are examples of *material needs*.

But people do not exist in isolation. We also need love and friendship and recognition from our fellows; we need to belong to groups and to feel that we belong, and we need to be aware of ourselves as persons in relation to surrounding social groups. These are *social needs*.

It is hard to tell which are the most important. If our material needs are not satisfied, we die from hunger or exposure; if our social needs are not satisfied, we are liable to suffer psychological problems. Now the crucial point is that in our consumption of goods we satisfy both material and social needs. Various social groups identify themselves through shared attitudes, manners, accents and habits of consumption — for instance through the clothes they wear. In this way the objects that we use and consume cease to be mere objects of use; they become carriers of information about what kind of people we are, or would like to be. In Barthes's words (1967: 41), the objects are *semanticized* (see further pp. 152-6). And this makes it possible for advertisers to exploit people's needs for group membership, self-identification, and so on. Whereas it is relatively easy to provide exact information about the material value of an article of clothing (as a function of its price and quality), any indication on the part of the advertiser that a particular article is associated with a particular social group is bound to be, if not untruthful, then at least unverifiable. This play on social values is obvious in the following example:

> The fast-moving world of
>   JOCKEY ®
> When the pace warms up, Jockey shirts
> stay cool. Cotton cool. Beautifully co-ordinated
> with Jockey briefs. Whatever you're getting into,
> and out of, it'll feel better — and look better —
> when it's Jockey.
> Underwear from 99p
> Tops from £2.25
> JOCKEY ®   by Lyle & Scott
>
> (*Reader's Digest*, April 1977)

The advert is illustrated with pictures of young men and women enjoying the good life on the Riviera: boating, horse-riding, playing tennis, drinking.

The only factual information we get is the price of the product and, partly, its ability to stay cool. Otherwise, the rest of the text suggests to the reader only that if he would like to belong in the fast-moving world, he should wear Jockey underwear and tops.

Clothing is a product group which satisfies both material and social needs, but we use lots of things which satisfy no material needs whatsoever. Reekie (1974: 22) observes about perfume that if our consumption was motivated solely by material needs, women would stop using perfume altogether. One social need satisfied by perfume could be satisfied equally well by the cheapest and most efficient deodorant, or by a wash. But women still use perfume — and one brand rather than another — because of the symbolic value of their particular brand. They define themselves, and are encouraged to define themselves, as persons through the brand of perfume which they use:

Rapport. They've got it. She wears it.

(*She*, October 1977)

In fact it is hard to see how commodities like perfume could be advertised at all in a purely informative and unpersuasive way.

THE FUNCTION OF ADVERTISING

In the preceding section we have argued that once a society has reached a stage where a reasonably large part of its population lives above subsistence level, advertising is inevitable, and that it is inevitably persuasive. This is true only with an important qualification, namely that the system with which we are dealing is a capitalist one.

A capitalist economy is divided into two parts: a sphere of production where commodities are produced, and a sphere or circulation where commodities and money are exchanged. In the sphere of production men are fundamentally unequal; there are those who own the means of production, capitalists, and those who do not, workers; in principle only the capitalists (majority shareholders) have any influence on what and how much is to be produced, although more often than not they may act on the advice of employees. In the sphere of circulation men are in principle free and equal; the commodity owner is free to decide whether to sell or not, to whom and at what price, and the potential buyer is free to buy or not. This is true even when the commodity is labour power; the worker is free to accept employment or not at the wage offered, and the industrialist is free to employ a worker or not. As advertising obviously has its place within the sphere of circulation, we shall discuss this sphere in somewhat greater detail.[2]

In a pre-capitalist system of direct exchange, or barter, individual producers, a farmer and a weaver perhaps, meet in the market-place; the farmer has been able to produce more corn than he needs, the weaver has been able to produce more linen than he needs, and by an act of mutual consent they exchange a certain amount of corn for a certain amount of linen.

There are two important points to notice about this transaction. First, the complete equality of the two parties in the transaction:

each possesses a product which only the other needs, which represents only exchange value to himself but use value to the other. Second, the products which they exchange become commodities only through the act of exchange, a commodity being a product which is produced with a special view to exchange. (Note the close similarity between the market-place in this situation and the classified advertising columns of a modern newspaper.)

Now let us turn to the act of exchange in a fully developed capitalist system. Here commodities are not the surplus products of individual producers. Rather, they are produced on a mass basis in factories in order to be sold to an anonymous market. The owner of the factory has made certain capital outlays on machinery, raw materials and workers' wages. When the commodity is sold, he has to get these outlays back plus a profit for reinvestment and private consumption.

The process of selling and buying in a developed capitalist system thus differs markedly from the market-place situation described above. In spite of the theoretical equality of men when they interact in the sphere of circulation, the manufacturer and his potential customer are in fact unequal (Haug 1971: 15). For the seller (and, in particular, the shareholder) the commodity represents no use value; he is interested in it only as a depository of exchange value which is realized through the sale of the commodity. For the buyer the commodity represents use value, but what he has to offer the seller in return is not something of use value to the seller but the embodiment of exchange value, money.

No one will want to buy a product unless it seems to be of use value to him, but since the seller's only interest in his commodity is selling it, he will be satisfied as long as the commodity *appears* to be of use value. The more attractive the product appears, the more people will want to buy it, and the shorter will be the lag between the time when the product leaves the factory and the time when the product is sold. This, according to Haug (ibid.), has led to an aestheticization of commodities (*Warenästhetik*). This aestheticization may be inherent in the product itself in the form of design (cars, for instance), smell (washing-up liquid), or colouring (beverages) — strictly irrelevant to the material use value of the product; it may appear in close connection with the product (the specially shaped bottles of beverages), or completely detached from the product, in the advertising. Not only does advertising help make products appear as aesthetically pleasing as possible, the advert becomes an aesthetic object in itself. As we shall see later (e.g. pp. 50-7, 152-6), this aestheticization of the advertising message means that adverts can profitably be analysed by means of techniques normally applied to verbal and visual art; advertising is in fact a 'sub-literary' genre (Leech 1969: 66).

In a situation where it is technologically possible for more firms to produce largely identical products, it is vital for each firm to provide a reason for the consumer to prefer its particular brand to those of its competitors, and even apologists of advertising admit that this may lead to 'wasteful product differentiation' (Harris and Seldon 1962: 236). The aestheticization of the product plays a major role in this differentiation as the well-known anecdote concerning competition between Ford and General Motors shows: when GM began to produce coloured Chevrolets, Henry Ford growled, 'You can have any colour you want, so long as it's black' — with disastrous results for Ford (Reekie 1974: 5-6). Later (pp. 154 ff.) we shall see that it is in fact not just the product but also the consumer that becomes aestheticized.

We have already pointed out that through the consumption of goods human beings satisfy both material and social needs. This we take to be a general feature not peculiar to capitalist societies. We further argued that once an advertiser wanted to claim any social use value for his product, he was bound to leave the area of factual information and enter the area of persuasion. Haug (1971: 65 ff.) now observes that along with the tendency to aestheticize, advertising has a tendency to disregard the material use value of commodities altogether. Instead of making claims, real or exaggerated, about the primary use value of his product, the advertiser will promise the consumer that the acquisition and consumption of his product will give youth, love, recognition, and so on. Haug refers to this as a corruption or distortion of use values. We shall return to the question of corrupted use values in chapters 5 and 6.

THE SCOPE OF THIS BOOK

In this book we shall investigate how the advertising message is

communicated. The main emphasis will be on the linguistic communication, but as illustrations are an important part of the overall
message, an analysis of the visual communication will often be
necessary. The most important techniques of analysis are explained
in chapter 2.

Although television is an extremely important advertising
medium,[3] we shall deal exclusively with press advertising. There
are two reasons for this: printed adverts are easier to store and easier
to study than TV adverts, and, secondly, since TV commercials
extend in time and make use of the combined effect of sound and
picture, it is only possible to give a very incomplete reproduction
of them in a book, whereas a printed advert can be reproduced as
a whole. On the one hand this concentration on press advertising
may not be a very great disadvantage, since there is no reason to
believe that TV and press advertising differ in their persuasive
methods in a basic way, although an analysis of TV adverts, owing
to the processual character of the TV commercial and its use of
both sound and picture, requires an additional body of analytical
procedures. On the other hand it does mean that some heavily advertised product groups, notably breakfast cereals and washing
powders, will be virtually absent from the analysis.

It is the job of advertising to influence consumers towards buying
the product, and it is a tenet of all propaganda that the propagan-
dist cannot create new needs but only retard or accelerate existing
trends (Brown 1963: 77). Therefore, if advertising agencies know
their job, advertising can be expected to reflect pretty closely the
current trends and value systems of a society. However, potential
buyers of motor-bikes will probably differ from the housewife on
the look-out for new cutlery, and this will presumably be reflected
in the values played on in each case. In other words, we may expect
the method of persuasion to vary with product type and the age,
sex and social class of the prospective reader. For this reason it is
important that a study of advertising should cover the widest possible
range of publications, while on the other hand it may be considered
reasonable to exclude special-interest magazines.

Accordingly, this study is based on advertising material from the
following publications (the information on circulation and readership is from the *National Readership Survey* 1976-77). Only display
advertisements are included. The material comprises one issue a

month of each publication covering the period April to October 1977. In addition, individual adverts have been quoted from various other British and American publications.

General

News of the World   This is by far the largest weekly publication with a circulation of about five million. About 80 per cent of its readers are working class, and about 50 per cent are under 35. It is read by approximately the same number of women and men.

The Sunday Times   The largest 'quality' Sunday newspaper, its circulation is about 1.3 million and 75 per cent of its readers are upper-middle and middle class.

Titbits   A middle-sized weekly magazine, circulation about 400,000. Its readership is predominantly working class (75 per cent).

Reader's Digest   The largest monthly magazine with a circulation of over 1.6 million. Its two largest readership groups are lower-middle class and upper-working class (28 and 32 per cent respectively). It is read by about 20 per cent of the population in the 15-64 age groups, but by only 13 per cent in the 65-plus group.

Women's magazines

Woman   One of the three largest women's weeklies with a circulation of over 1.4 million (the two others are *Woman's Own* and *Women's Weekly*). Of its readers, 59 per cent are working class, 27 per cent are lower-middle class, and 14 per cent upper and middle-middle class. It is read by between 18 and 35 per cent of the women in all age groups, although, judging from its editorial material, it caters mainly for the housewife. Of its female readers, 82 per cent are married; just over 50 per cent of its female readers are also employed outside the home (full time or part time). Furthermore, 16 per cent of its readers are men.

She   A monthly magazine with a circulation of about 300,000. Its three largest readership groups are the middle-middle class

(20 per cent), the lower-middle class (34 per cent), and the upper-working class (26 per cent). To judge from its editorial material, it caters mainly for the married middle-class women who are also (or would also like to be) employed outside the home.[4] Of its female readers, 60 per cent in fact work part time or full time, and 78 per cent are married. They typically come from the age groups up to 54 years; in the 55-plus age groups, its readership declines steeply. In addition, 25 per cent of its readers are men.

Cosmopolitan   A monthly magazine with a circulation of about 410,000. As *She* is seen by an average of 5.9 persons per copy and *Cosmopolitan* only by 3.6 persons, their average readership per issue is about the same. In terms of social class their readership profiles are virtually identical, but *Cosmopolitan* is a much more glossy magazine than *She*. The editorial material would suggest that its typical reader is the single middle-class woman. In fact, 48 per cent of its female readers are unmarried, and 72 per cent of all its readers come from the age group 15-34. As many as 30 per cent of all its readers are men.

Men's magazines

Mayfair   In our culture women are more conscious of being women than men are of being men (Millum 1975: 71), and this is reflected in the virtual absence of men's magazines compared to the wide variety of publications for women. Apart from special interest magazines, the only men's magazines are all more or less pornographic. With a circulation of about 276,000, *Mayfair* is one of the larger of these. Of its readers, 64 per cent are under 35; its largest readership groups are lower-middle class (24 per cent), upper-working class (41 per cent) and middle-working class (22 per cent).

2

Language and Communication

Advertising men who want to avoid the less pleasant overtones of the name of their trade like to refer to themselves as 'communicators' (Norins 1966: 5), and advertising is of course a form of communication. This, however, is an extremely broad concept, and to get a more precise idea of what it includes we shall look at some activities that are covered by the term. There are three major distinctions to make.

Verbal and non-verbal communication

This distinction refers to whether or not language is used. Language is our most important vehicle of communication, but even when we talk to each other, our speech is accompanied by gestures and poses by which we communicate non-verbally. The simultaneous use of verbal and non-verbal communication is an extremely important element in our culture. We find it in plays, films, television, strip cartoons, and in most advertising.

Public and private communication

This distinction has to do with the communication situation. Private communication is a process which involves a known number of persons who are all known to each other, as in a conversation between friends or in letter writing. In public communication the situation is more complicated: one type is addressed simply to an anonymous public — newspaper articles, novels, plays, films, advertising — but in another type a known number of persons are at the same time communicating *with* each other and *to* an anonymous public; this is the situation of parliamentary debates and radio or TV discussions.

One-way and two-way communication

There is a strong tendency for this distinction to be identical with the previous one: in private communication the participants take turns at being speaker and listener, writer and reader, whereas in most types of public communication there is one speaker/writer addressing an anonymous public who cannot answer him back. Public two-way communication occurs typically, and normally, in public debates, whereas private one-way communication, although it may occur, is always regarded as abnormal and socially un- acceptable — we do not like being lectured to in private.

Advertising, then, is verbal/non-verbal, public, one-way com- munication. Note that these properties are common to advertising and most forms of popular entertainment, such as films, television and strip cartoons.

We noted that the communication situation of public debates is complex in two respects, (a) with regard to the number of people addressed, and (b) with regard to the one-way/two-way distinction. In art similar complexities are made use of. Consider a film or a novel: the entire work of art is the artist's communication to his audience, that is, a case of public one-way communication; but within the work there will be dialogues between the characters, that is, private two-way communication, where the characters are addressing each other, although, in actual fact, the artist is still addressing the audience. Below (pp. 50-7) we shall see cases in which advertising makes use of the same device.

THE VERBAL MESSAGE

In the study of communication the object of study (what goes on between the participants in the communication process) is referred to as a text. A dinner-party conversation, a novel, a film or an adver- tisement are thus all considered texts in this sense of the word.

In the study of texts we can take the following three observations for granted:

The text exists in a particular communication situation.
The text is a structured unit — it has texture.
The text communicates meaning.

Thus any text can, and should be studied from three points of view: How does it function in the communication situation? How is it textured, that is, how are its parts united into a whole? What meaning does it communicate?

The communication situation

Communication necessarily involves at least two persons, the person speaking (the *addresser*) and the person spoken to (the *addressee*). In the process of communication *meaning* is transmitted between the two participants. However, meaning cannot be transmitted in the abstract; it must be embodied in some *code* (the meaning 'stop', for instance, can be transmitted through various codes: a red and white road sign, a policeman's arm, the red light in traffic lights, or the word *stop*). In order for anything to be communicated at all, addresser and addressee further have to be in contact with each other, that is, the message has to be communicated through some kind of *channel* (in conversation, sound waves; in writing, letters on paper; the sound waves may be converted into other forms of waves as in the telephone, radio or television). Finally, any act of communication takes place in a situation, a *context*; this involves the situation in which addresser and addressee are placed, including the immediately preceding events, but context also includes the wider cultural context of the addresser and addressee, and the knowledge which they share about their total situation and their culture.

The figure on page 16 is a graphic representation of the communication situation (cf. Leech 1974: 49). In the case of advertising the relation between this abstract, general communication model and the actual situation is fairly obvious: the addresser is the advertiser, and the addressee is the reader, the meaning transmitted is about the product (more specifically, an attempt to make the reader buy the product), the code (in the case of press advertising) is language and some sort of visual code (see below pp. 32-48), the channel consists of printed publications, and the context will include such features as the reader's total situation (does he have the product already? can he afford it? etc.), the publication in which the advertisement appears, and last but not least the knowledge that the text is an advert (note that if an advert looks too much like the editorial material of the publication, the word 'advertisement' is usually printed above it. See plate 6.

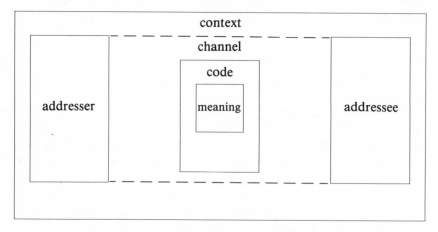

In communication, language can perform a variety of functions. We use language to express our emotions, to inform our interlocutors of facts of which they were not previously aware, to influence people's actions or thoughts, to talk about language, to chat with friends about nothing in particular, or to tell stories and make jokes. Interestingly, each function can be related directly to one of the components in the communication model.[1]

In the *expressive* function, language focuses on the addresser, his feelings, wishes, attitudes and will. This is the function we use when we assert ourselves as individuals. To condemn, apologize, forgive, approve, praise and reprimand are examples of expressive communicative acts (or speech acts; cf. Searle 1969, 1971).

In the *directive* function, language is oriented towards the addressee. Here language is used to influence the addressee's actions, emotions, beliefs and attitudes. To persuade, advise, recommend, exhort, invite, permit, order, compel, warn and threaten are examples of directive speech acts.

The *informational* function focuses on the meaning. When we convey to our interlocutor information which he did not possess already, or when we ask for information, we use language informationally. To inform, report, describe, assert, declare, maintain, request, confirm and refute are informational speech acts.

The *metalingual* function focuses on the code. In this function language is used to talk about language, that is, utterances like '"controversy" should be pronounced with the stress on the first syllable'.

The *interactional* function has to do with the channel. Here language is used to create, maintain and finish contact between addresser and addressee. This function is especially important if the interlocutors are not in visual contact with each other as in a telephone conversation. The function of most casual conversation is also interactional: people will talk about the weather not because they have important information to convey, but because it is considered inappropriate not to say anything.

The *contextual* function relates to the context. Apart from a few formulaic expressions — such as 'The court is now in session' or 'The court stands adjourned for ten minutes' — whose sole function is to create or cancel a context, it is hard to think of any longer utterances with a purely contextual function. But there are a number of words whose meaning is defined exclusively by reference to the elements in the communication process: 'I', 'we', 'you', 'this', 'that', 'here', 'there', 'now', and 'then' point to aspects of the situation, and have a different meaning in each situation. These words are often referred to as *deictic*, and their function is to *anchor* the text in a concrete situation. Below (pp. 34-5) we shall see that an important difference between the verbal and the visual medium is that the latter lacks such deictic anchoring devices (for the concept of deictic anchorage, see Rommetveit 1968: 185 ff.).

The poetic function is oriented towards the code and the meaning simultaneously: the code is used in a special way in order to communicate meaning that could not otherwise be communicated. The special 'poetic' use of the code is of course most obvious when such well-known poetic devices as rhyme, rhythm and metaphor are made use of, but these features need not be present for the use of language to be poetic. The complex situation which arises when a piece of apparent private communication is embedded in a piece of actual public communication (see above p. 14) is another example of the special poetic use of language. Note that the complex communication situation along with the use of poetic devices like metaphor means that the message becomes ambiguous. When we read poetry (and other artistic linguistic products), we constantly have to ask questions like 'Who is addressing whom?' and 'What is the meaning of this particular metaphor?'

Textual structure

Cohesion and coherence

We have stated that it can be taken for granted that the text is a structured unit. This may not always be true without qualifications, but what is true is that the reader/listener works under this assumption that until he is proved wrong. Our understanding of what has gone before in the text is continually seen in the light of what comes after, and if inconsistencies arise, we try to modify our interpretation in order to create structure rather than discard the text as incoherent.

Consider now the following example:

(1) The bill is large.

In isolation this sentence is ambiguous; it may refer either to the size of the sheet of paper or to the amount to be paid. But in the context of (2) the sentence ceases to be ambiguous:

(2) The bill is large, but it need not be paid.

From a grammatical point of view there is no reason why 'the bill' shouldn't refer to a sheet of paper in (2) as well as in (1), but it simply does not make sense to say that there is some sort of contrast between the two statements 'the bill is large' and 'it need not be paid' unless 'bill' is interpreted as 'sum', and the presence of 'but' indicates that the two statements *are* in contrast.

We can talk about textual structure at two levels. On the one hand, example (2) consists of two sentences conjoined by means of the co-ordinating conjunction 'but', which indicates that the two are in contrast and that each is surprising seen in the light of the other. The two sentences are further linked by a recurrent element, 'the bill' — in its second occurrence represented by the pronoun 'it' — and this element is the subject of both sentences. English sentences can be linked in various ways, among which repetition of an element and back reference by means of pronouns are among the more important (see Halliday and Hasan, 1976). Following Widdowson (1973), we shall refer to this kind of formal linkage between sentences as *cohesion* (cf. also Widdowson 1978: 24 ff.).

At another level, no matter how closely we analyse the formal cohesion between sentences, we shall not get anywhere near to an answer to such questions as why only the interpretation 'sum' makes sense in (2). To answer this type of question we shall have to look at the logical structure of texts. We have seen that 'but' denotes a contrast between the two sentences in (2). The nature of this contrast is not mentioned explicitly, but we may assume a shared knowledge between speaker and listener which enables them to establish a succession of links between the two constituent sentences. In our interpretation of the text we can reconstruct this shared knowledge:

'the bill is large' —this is unpleasant, since it means that we shall
                        have to pay a large amount of money;
'but'   nevertheless there is no need to worry, for
'it need not be paid.'

This inner, logical linkage in texts will be referred to as *coherence*.

It is by no means always the case that a text is both cohesive and coherent as in the case of (2). In fact, as (3) is intended to show, communication would be enormously complicated if we always had to make explicit the formal links between the parts of a piece of discourse:

(3) Husband: Mother is arriving from Birmingham at 3.50.
     Wife: I have an appointment with the dentist.
     Husband: OK.

This is an example of a perfectly normal, successful and coherent conversation. We are not in doubt that the two parties have understood each other, and that the result will be that the husband will pick up his mother at the station. Yet there is absolutely nothing to mark the formal cohesion between each remark. If we try and fill in the missing formal and logical links between each remark, we see readily why communication would be a cumbersome process if we always had to be explicit:

(3a) Husband: Mother is arriving from Birmingham at 3.50.
              One of us will have to collect her at the station, will you do it?

> Wife: I'm afraid I cannot do it, for I have an
>   appointment with the dentist.
> Husband: That's OK. I'll collect her then.

While it is thus perfectly normal for a text to be coherent without
being cohesive, we should always be suspicious of cases where the
outer, formal cohesion is not matched by inner, semantic coherence:
in that situation the form of language may be used to cover up for
a break in the logical structure of an argument. This is a common
ingredient of 'loaded language', and is quite frequent in advertising.
The general effect of this technique is that we are led to believe that
the text says things which it could not say explicitly:

(4) **If only you could see through some other soaps.**
    The pure amber transparency of Pears soap shows
    you why it is different from any other soap you
    can buy.
    Pears *is* pure soap, free from additives that
    could cause harm to delicate skin.

(She, October 1977)

On the face of it there is nothing remarkable about this text. It is
only when we take a closer look at the logical connection — the
coherence — between the two paragraphs of the copy that we notice
that something is wrong. The first paragraph contains a dependent
interrogative clause ('why it is different') indicating that there are
reasons for the difference between Pears soap and other brands,
and the second paragraph consists of an emphatic statement about
a characteristic quality of the product ('Pears *is* pure soap'). The
link between the two which our normal experience with language
would naturally lead us to supply is this: 'Pears soap is different
from any other soap you can buy *because* . . .' In other words, Pears
is the only soap which is pure and free from additives which could
harm delicate skin. For obvious reasons the advertisement cannot
make this claim explicitly: in the first place it would be impossible
to substantiate, and hence illegal (see the *Trade Descriptions Act
1968*); secondly, it would be considered unethical according to
professional standards.[2]

Information structure

The concepts of cohesion and coherence deal with how sentences are connected to make up a text. But textual structure can also be studied from the point of view of the structuring of information *within* the sentences. We are thus concerned with a view of the sentence which regards it as consisting not of subjects, objects and verbs, but rather of units of information which can be positioned in various ways relative to each other, whereby varying degrees of prominence are attached to them. Under the heading of information structure, we deal with the following pairs of concepts (cf. Halliday 1970: 160-4):

theme — rheme
given — new
non-focal — focal

Theme is what the sentence talks about, *rheme* is what is said about it. In unmarked cases the theme is the subject of the sentence, while the rest of the sentence is rheme.

Given is the information which is assumed to be known in the verbal or non-verbal context, that is, items of information which have either been explicitly referred to in the text or can be taken for granted in the context. *New* is the new information that is supplied in the sentence. In unmarked cases given information coincides with the theme, and new information falls within the rheme.

The *focal* element is the informationally most prominent member of a tone group (which, for present purposes, we can regard as equivalent to sentence). This element is marked off by a characteristic accent, the nuclear accent, which in normal cases falls on the last stressed syllable of the tone group (Halliday, 1967). The focal element of a sentence is thus the element which contains the most prominent new information.

Let us now imagine a situation where someone has asked me what I gave John for his birthday. A natural reply would be

(5) I gave John a **book**.

(**Bold type** denotes nuclear accent.)
In this sentence 'I' is the theme (the sentence is about what *I* did), and 'gave John a book' is the rheme (*what* I did). In the situation

both 'I', 'gave' and 'John' are given, since all three have been mentioned in the question, and the only new information supplied is thus 'a book', which, accordingly, receives the nuclear accent.

Suppose now, instead, that someone has asked me what I have done with a book which I had borrowed from him. My reply might be:

(6) I gave the book to **John**.

Again, 'I' is theme, and 'gave the book to John' is rheme. As in the previous example, 'I' and 'gave' are given, but 'book' and 'John' have changed places: this time 'book' is given (and is accordingly referred to as 'the' book rather than 'a' book), and only 'John' is new. Since the final position in the sentence is normally the position reserved for the most prominent element, 'John' this time is placed there.

However, I could equally appropriately have given the following answer:

(7) I gave **John** the book.

Here *John* is still the only new information, but it has been moved away from the final position, while retaining the nuclear accent. Whenever the element carrying the nuclear accent occupies a position other than the final position, we talk about marked focus, and the effect of moving the focal element out of its normal position is to make it more emphatic. While (7) and (6) thus both refer to the same fact, and might be uttered in the same situation, (7) states more emphatically than (6) that it is John, and not Mary or Louise, who now has the book.

It has often been observed that advertising copy has a tendency to chop up sentences into shorter bits by using full stops where ordinary prose would use commas or no punctuation at all. Leech (1966: 90-7, 113-16, 148-50, 170-4) refers to this phenomenon as 'disjunctive syntax'. In the sixties this 'jazzy' or 'trendy' style was used to such an extent that it must have been considered to have an associative value of its own. Today the technique is used far less extensively, but it still survives, and we are now in a position to observe one of its communicative effects:

(8a) . . . an automatic applicator gently smooths on soft creme or high-shine colour, for a smooth silky finish that lasts. And lasts.

(8b) . . . colours that look lastingly tempting. Longer.

(Cosmopolitan, July 1977)

Both extracts, taken from the same advert, contain examples of 'incomplete' sentences: in (a) 'And lasts.' and in (b) 'Longer.', and in both cases we are dealing with an element which might have functioned as a constituent of the preceding sentence, but which has been separated from the sentence by means of a full stop. The effect of this is to cut up the sentence into more information units, so that the same sequence of words will contain two focal elements rather than one. Thus in (a) each occurrence of the word 'lasts' would carry the nuclear accent (cf. '. . . a smooth silky finish that lasts and lasts'), and in (b) it becomes possible to place a nuclear accent on both 'lastingly tempting' and 'longer' ('. . . colours that look lastingly tempting longer').

Content

As we have tried to show in the two preceding sections, both the particular communicative function of language employed and the internal structuring of the text contribute to the total meaning of the text. Of course, the most decisive contribution comes from what the text actually talks about, that is, from the words that are used (it is for this reason that we distinguish between meaning and content). We shall not here go into a discussion of the use of vocabulary in advertising (though we do look at some questions of vocabulary on pp. 67-70), so what we are offering is firstly a description of how content can be communicated both explicitly and by implication, and then some techniques for describing the larger content structures of texts.

Implicit and explicit content

All communication rests on the principle that nothing would be said unless there was some reason for saying it, and this 'good reason' principle enables us to make a number of legitimate deductions from what we hear (or read). In other words it is necessary to distinguish between what is actually said and what follows from either the content of what is said or from the mere fact that it is said. On the basis of the relative degree of certainty with which such deductions are made, it is possible to distinguish between three degrees of implicit content: entailment, presupposition and expectation (cf. Leech 1974: 291-301).

Entailment is what one can logically conclude from a statement. Thus

> (9a) John left two minutes ago.

entails

> (9b) John is not here now.

Presupposition is what necessarily has to be the case for an utterance to be meaningful at all. Thus (9a) presupposes

> (9c) John was here two minutes ago.

Similarly

> (10a) When did you stop beating your wife?

presupposes

> (10b) There was a time when you were in the habit of beating your wife.

In other words, anybody who utters (10a) takes the truth of (10b) for granted, and it is impossible to answer (10a) directly without accepting (10b). Note also that it is much easier to deny a direct assertion than it is to deny presuppositions. Thus if somebody accuses me of beating my wife by saying, 'You sometimes beat your wife', I can deny the assertion by saying 'Of course I don't' or 'That's a lie'; but if somebody asks me the question of (10a), and I do not accept its presupposition, I can only make this clear to him by refusing to answer the question and saying something like, 'Now look here, this is an absurd question: I have never beaten my wife, and this is in fact what you're suggesting.'

Expectation builds on the 'good reason' principle. Whenever something is said, we assume that there must have been some reason for saying it. The reason can be that what is said is not always the case, that the addressee would not have been aware of certain facts unless they were pointed out to him, and so on.

(11a) Nobody in our department knows more about socio-linguistics than John.

expects

(11b) John knows more about socio-linguistics than all (or most) other people in our department.

In a situation where a student of mine has asked me to supervise a socio-linguistics paper, and I answer him by uttering (11a), the student would legitimately take my statement to mean that I am referring him to a colleague, John, since the normal rules of expectation would have led him to infer (11b) from (11a). To see that this is so, one need only imagine how the student would react if later I pointed out that all I had actually said about John was

(11c) John knows as much about socio-linguistics as everybody else in the department.

In ordinary discourse, anybody who has uttered (11a) but claims that he only meant (11c) would be considered to be quibbling.

The normal rules of expectation probably only apply fully in the informational and directive functions of language. In the interactional function, they are certainly suspended. When we say 'Nice morning' or 'Long time no see', we are not assuming that our interlocutor needs to be made aware of these facts.

In advertising language, which almost by definition has to make as many positive claims as possible for the product without actually making them, the use of presupposition and expectation is an extremely frequent feature. Consider the following headlines:

(12a) Which of these continental quilt patterns will suit your bedroom best?

(*Reader's Digest*, September 1977)

which presupposes

(12b) All these continental quilt patterns will suit your bedroom.

and

(12c) One of these continental quilt patterns will suit your bedroom better than the others.

Secondly,

(13a) Why more and more men are turning to Flora
                                    (*Reader's Digest*, April 1977)

which presupposes

(13b) More and more men are turning to Flora.

The reason for this use of headlines which presuppose rather than assert the content of the statements which we have cited as (12b), (12c) and (13b) lies in what we said above about the difference between assertion and presupposition: it is much easier to question or deny an assertion than a presupposition.

The play on expectation in advertising language is perhaps slightly less conspicuous than presupposition, but at least as common and well attested by professional advertising men critical of the standards of their trade (see Stevens 1972: 26-74; Wight 1972: 46-88).

One type consists of a sentence containing a negative word and an adjective in the comparative. This type is comparable to the example in (11) above:

(14a) Beauty wise, value wise, you can't buy better than Rimmel.
                                    (*She*, October 1977)

expects

(14b) Rimmel is the best you can buy.

although it 'actually' asserts only

(14c) Rimmel is as good as anything else you can buy.

In fact, whenever a negation is used to claim that the product is free of some undesirable characteristics, such a claim makes sense only because rules of expectation permit us to deduce that competing products do have these characteristics. This is true of the standard 'no belts no loops' claim for various kinds of sanitary protection as well as of the following:

(15a) [X] is the light moisturizing cream.
It's not greasy or sticky.

(Cosmopolitan, July 1977)

which expects

(15b) Other moisturizing creams are greasy and sticky.

In the case of positive claims, the good-reason principle will often lead us to expect that if a specific claim is made for a product, this must be because the product differs from competitors in this respect. For example, if an advert for a brand of pain-killer mentions, say, solubility several times, there must be some reason for mentioning it, and the expectation is:

(16) No other pain-killers are soluble.

which is untrue.

Participant roles

In the communication situation of advertising there are three main participants: the advertiser, the product and the prospective buyer. One of the questions with which we are concerned in this book is how each of these are characterized in advertising texts and how this characterization varies with such factors as the sex and social class of readers (see chapter 4).

In his book *Sémantique structurale* (1966),[3] A. J. Griemas discusses various models for the analysis of the content structure of texts. Of particular interest is the so-called *actantial* model, which was originally devised as a tool for the analysis of folktales and myths.

According to Greimas, narratives can be analysed in terms of three fundamental pairs of *actants* and the relations between them:

subject — object
helper — opponent
giver — receiver

The *subject* (the hero) strives after some desired *object* (a princess, honour, wealth, freedom); in his endeavours he is opposed by the *opponent* (the villain, a dragon, an ogre) and assisted by the *helper* (his followers, a fairy); finally the *giver* (normally someone of higher status than the subject — the king, for instance) steps in and gives the object to the *receiver* (the ultimate beneficiary, either the hero or someone else — e.g. his people). The actants are abstract roles which, in the concrete narrative, are represented by concrete *actors*. Greimas schematizes the model in the following way (by way of illustration we have added the actors from the Robin Hood myth):

GIVER ⟶ OBJECT ⟶ RECEIVER
(King Richard)   (freedom/justice)   (the people)

↑

HELPER ⟶ SUBJECT ⟵ OPPONENT
(the merry men)   (Robin Hood)   (Prince John)

Let us now try and apply this model to a piece of actual advertising copy:

(17) **The Sanatogen Smile.**
Vitamins are essential to good health. In theory,
you should be able to get all the vitamins you need
from a properly balanced diet.
  Sometimes though, if you're particularly busy, you
5 may only have a snack lunch. Which of course, may only
have snack vitamins. If you're on a diet and eating less
calories, you could also be eating less vitamins. Reheating food at lunchtime can reduce the vitamin content.
  And of course, if you cut out a meal, you cut out every-
10 thing that goes with it as well. Sanatogen Multivitamins
give you essential vitamins and minerals that help to
ensure good health. So take one Sanatogen tablet every
morning and be sure of getting the vitamins and minerals
you need to last you through the day. Have you got the
15 Sanatogen Smile?
Sanatogen multivitamins
One a day, everyday, for positive health.
(*Reader's Digest*, April 1977)

The advert consists of a *headline*, *body copy*, and a *slogan* (plus an illustration which need not concern us here). The words of the headline recur as the focal element of the last sentence of the body copy ('the Sanatogen Smile'), and the focal element of the first sentence is repeated in a variant form as the final element of the slogan ('good health' — 'positive health'). There is thus no doubt that good health and its symbol, the 'Sanatogen Smile', is the desired object which is sought for by the subject 'you'. In his/her quest for good health the subject is assisted by the helper, 'vitamins and minerals that help to ensure good health'. The opponent is represented by the forces which may result in an insufficient vitamin content — a snack lunch, a diet, reheating food, cutting out a meal. Finally, the giver and the receiver are represented by the product and 'you' respectively — 'Sanatogen Multivitamins *give* you essential vitamins and minerals'.

This example is typical in its representation of the actantial roles, although the distribution of roles is perhaps more obvious than in most adverts. Of particular interest are the facts that the role of object is not filled by the product but by some quality or state associated with it, and that the consumer (the 'you') is both subject and receiver. Advertising, in other words, does not try to tell us that we need its products as such, but rather that the products can help us obtain something else which we do feel that we need. What that something is will be discussed in chapters 5 and 6.

The actantial model is a model for the analysis of the content structure of texts. It looks upon a text as consisting of relations between roles (actants). There are interesting parallels between this model and the grammatical theory known as *case grammar* (see Fillmore, 1968, 1971; Anderson, 1977), which looks upon sentences as consisting of relations between roles, with the relations expressed by verbs (and adjectives and prepositions) and the roles expressed by nouns. What motivated case grammar was the observation that an analysis of sentences in terms of subject—verb—object—adverbial reveals nothing about the meaning of sentences. In a sentence like 'the chemist dissolved the metal in the acid', the subject denotes the person who carries out the action (Agentive), the object is the entity affected by the action (Objective), and the adverbial prepositional phrase is the entity used in carrying out the action (Instrumental). In 'the acid dissolved the metal', it is the Instrumental which occurs as subject. Finally, the subject is Objective in 'the metal dissolved [in the acid]'.

As a consequence of observations like these, case grammarians have suggested that we should operate with a model of the sentence in which the relations between sentence elements — their case roles — are characterized directly. The problem now consists in setting up an inventory of case roles which is at once sufficiently detailed and sufficiently general for the description of texts. Unfortunately, there is no final version of case grammar, but for practical purposes the following inventory is serviceable:

agentive (agt.)	A person or being instigating an action: '*John* felled the tree.'
instrumental (ins.)	An object or force which is causally involved in the action: 'John felled the tree with *an axe*;' '*the pollution of the river* has killed the fish;' '*the explosion* rocked the building.'
dative (dat.)	A person or being who owns or receives something: '*John* has a dog;' *John* received a present;' 'Peter gave *John* a book.'
experiencer (exp.)	The person or being who has a feeling or receives a sense impression: '*Peter* saw the film;' '*John* believes that the earth is flat;' 'the film pleased *Peter*.'
factitive (fact.)	What comes into existence as a result of the action/process/event: 'Peter made *a table*;' 'John wrote *a letter*;' 'their diplomacy resulted *in war*.'
objective (obj.)	The person/entity which is affected by the action or is passively involved: 'Peter felled *the tree*/killed *John*;' 'Peter has *a dog*/saw *the film*;' '*the film* pleased Peter.' Most object clauses can also be analysed as obj.: 'Peter believes *that the earth is flat*.'
locative (loc.)	The place where something is situated or a process occurs:

'The department is *in these buildings*;'
'the department occupies *these buildings*;'
'*these buildings* contain the department.'

Since the actantial model and case grammar are essentially concerned with the same thing, though at different levels (the text and the sentence respectively), we will expect there to be correlations between an actantial analysis and a case analysis of a text. It would be reasonable to expect, for instance, that the subject is frequently expressed as agt. or exp., that the object is obj., ins. or fact., that the giver is agt., that the receiver is dat. or exp., that the helper is agt. or ins., and that the opponent is agt. Systematic deviations from these hypotheses must somehow be significant. Similarly, we must be on the look-out for instances where case roles and the semantic make-up of words do not match, for example instances where things occur in the agt. role or persons occur as obj.

Let us now return to the Sanatogen advert. The case roles of the actors — good health/the Sanatogen smile (object), you (subject/receiver), vitamins and minerals (helper), a snack lunch/reheating food, etc. (opponent), Sanatogen (giver) — are displayed below together with the verbs with which they play the respective roles. A dash before the verb indicates that the noun is the grammatical subject, a dash after the verb indicates that it is the object. Line numbers are added in parentheses.

good health/ the Sanatogen smile	fact.	essential to— (1), ensure— (12), for— (17)
	obj.	have got— (14)
you	dat.	—get (2,13), —need (2,14), give— (11), last— (14), —have got (14)
	agt.	—are busy (4), —have a snack lunch (5), —are on a diet (6), —eat (6,7), —re-heat (8-9), — cut out (9 *bis*), —take (12)
	exp.	—be sure (13)
vitamins and minerals	obj.	—are essential (1), get— (2,13), need— (2,14), have— (6), eat— (7), reduce— (8), give you— (11), —last (14)

	agt.	—help (11)
snack lunch, etc.	obj.	may have— (5), cut out— (9)
	dat.	—may have (5)
	ins.	—can reduce (8)
Sanatogen	agt.	—give (11)
	obj.	take— (12)

(In a couple of fairly uncontroversial cases, we have supplied a deleted nominal: e.g. '[you] take one Sanatogen tablet' (12), '[vitamins and minerals] to last you through the day' (14).)

The case roles of the object and the subject/receiver accord quite well with the hypothesis: 'good health' emerges as a result of the combined efforts of the subject, giver and helper, and is the object that the subject/receiver wishes to possess. Similarly, 'you' occurs in the roles of dat., agt. and exp., as we would expect of the subject/receiver. 'Vitamins and minerals', on the other hand, occur only once in the case role (agt.) which we would expect of a helper, but several times in the objective case, a role characteristic of things. The reason for this is, of course, that in spite of its role of helper, the word 'vitamins' does after all stand for the product advertised. The analysis of case roles thus shows that the product is treated as an object to a larger extent than we might expect from the actantial analysis. The opponent — 'snack lunch', etc. — also turns up in unexpected case roles. Note, however, that the actual opponent is not snack lunches or meals as such, but having snack lunches and cutting out meals. Here, the elements which actantial analysis deals with on the textual level are simply not accessible to analysis on the sentence level. Finally, it must be pointed out that although opponent and giver are not mentioned as frequently as subject, object, receiver and helper, this text is in fact quite unusual in that it mentions them at all. The central participants of most advertising copy are the subject/receiver (you), the helper (the product) and the object (some quality associated with the product).

THE VISUAL MESSAGE

We have already mentioned that the combination of verbal text and pictures has become increasingly important in our culture. But the importance of this combination can hardly be said to be reflected in the amount of research in it. Whereas on the one hand there is a large and reasonably well-grounded body of linguistic technique for the study of verbal texts to proceed from, and on the other there is a long and venerable tradition for the study of pictures in isolation (viz. in the history of art), research into mass-communicated, industrially produced texts combining verbal and visual elements is still only beginning to emerge. What we have to say in this section is thus bound to be fairly tentative. The section will focus on two topics: the relation between text and picture, and the ways in which we communicate by means of images, i.e. the relation between images and the content they communicate.

Text and picture

Consider plate 1. This is a picture of a man and a woman (the then President Carter and Mrs Thatcher) who are talking to each other. Or rather he is talking to her, and she seems to be listening attentively.

Plate 1   *'Howdy!' — President Carter and Mrs Thatcher*
News of the World *September 1977*

Let us now try and look at images as communication and see how visual communication differs from verbal communication. Let us say, for the sake of the argument, that the picture of President Carter and Mrs Thatcher is equivalent to the verbal message

(18) Last week Mrs Thatcher met President Carter in Washington.

The most important difference between the picture and the (verbal) text is that the text contains a verb in a definite tense-form. Whenever we say something, we are forced to make a choice between the tense and aspectual forms available in the language ('meets', 'is meeting', 'met', 'was meeting', 'has met', 'has been meeting', etc.). In contrast, images are tenseless. As we pointed out above (p. 17), language is able to refer to its own context by means of the phenomenon known as deixis, and tense is a deictic category (cf. Lyons 1977: 677-90), since tense is one of the means by which we indicate whether the event or state referred to in an utterance is regarded as simultaneous with or prior to the time at which the utterance is made.

As tense is an obligatory category, time deixis is practically never absent from an utterance. Place and person deixis, on the other hand, are optional in language: an utterance may or may not refer to its own location ('here') and addresser/addressee ('I', 'you'). But in pictures, these deictic categories too are always missing, and the deictic anchorage which is of vital importance for the correct interpretation of a verbal message is thus always absent in an image. For this reason, Barthes (1964) points out that images are ambiguous or polysemic, where verbal messages are (or at least can be) unambiguous or monosemic.

When text and picture co-occur in the printed media, the most frequent relation between them is what Barthes (ibid.) refers to as *anchorage*. The meaning of this term should be clear by now: the text (a caption, say) provides the link between the picture and the situation in space and time which cannot be established through purely visual means of expression. (In fact, Barthes meant the term to cover not just deictic anchorage, but anything in the text which anchors the picture in reality and helps us to interpret it.) At the same time, the text also selects one of several possible interpretations of the picture, and for this reason it is true to say that whereas a picture in itself is always neutral, a picture with a caption never is.

The caption to the Carter—Thatcher picture goes like this:

(19) HOWDY: President Carter interrupts a hectic schedule to welcome Mrs Thatcher to Washington.

Some of the information given in this caption is clearly anchoring: we are informed about the identity of the two persons depicted (henceforth, the *actors*), and we are told that the place is Washington. There is no reference to the time, but the fact that Mrs Thatcher had just returned from a trip to America could probably be taken as general background knowledge at the time the paper appeared.

In the Carter—Thatcher example the verb in the anchoring caption is in the simple present tense ('interrupts'). When, as in this case, a verb expressing an event is used in the simple present, it typically denotes an event simultaneous with the present moment. This is the use of the simple present which we find in sports commentaries, for instance ('Walker *swings* a right at the West Indian' — see Leech 1971: 2), and this meaning of the simple present has been carried over to newspaper headlines and captions (Leech 1971: 8). A much more frequent meaning of the simple present tense in anchoring advertising texts is the 'eternal truth' variety ('the sun *rises* in the east'). This type is illustrated in

(20) A diamond is forever.

(*Ms Magazine*, May 1977)

which occurs as a slogan under a picture of a young couple. They are embracing, and a diamond ring is visible on the girl's left hand.

Barthes (1968) refers to the other main functions of text in relation to picture as *relay*. The typical instance of this occurs in the speech balloons of comic strips. Unlike anchorage, relay denotes a reciprocal relation between text and picture, in that each contributes its own part of the overall message. In the case of (19), the word 'howdy' could be taken as an instance of relay, as we are presumably meant to understand that this is what Carter is saying. But note that this is not a pure case of relay. The word 'howdy' also directs our interpretation of the picture, so that we understand it as referring to a welcoming scene. Another newspaper might equally well have used the same photo to show its readers how Carter warned Mrs Thatcher against endangering East—West negotiations by ill-considered public announcements. Inevitably, there is a strong element of anchorage even in what purports to be a clear example of relay. This is true of virtually all captions to press photos, and of advertising texts apart from the relatively rare cases where an advert takes the form of a strip cartoon (see plate 11).

Images and communication

No one would deny that images communicate, but the trouble is that this fact does not warrant the conclusion that images can be analysed in ways analogous to the procedures of analysis applied to the means of communication *par excellence* — language (Eco 1976: 213 ff.). Outside such highly conventionalized subcodes as road signs, it is not possible to analyse images in terms corresponding to the sentences, words, morphemes and phonemes of language.

Icon, index and symbol

If something can be used to communicate, it is because it can stand for something else. In linguistics, and in the more general discipline of semiotics, the 'stand-for' function is customarily referred to as the *sign* function. Peirce (1960: 156-73) distinguishes three types of relation between a sign and its object (what it stands for), viz. the iconic, the indexical and the symbolic relation.

In an *icon* the relation between sign and object is natural or motivated. This means that in some culturally relevant respect the sign strikes us as similar to its object. The similarity may range from shared physical properties (as in the case of a toy gun representing a real gun) to a remote similarity of use (a broomstick can represent a horse, because both can be straddled, cf. Gombrich 1963: 1-11). In the same way, the similarity may depend on convention to a greater or lesser extent: a circle encompassing three lines and a curve may represent a smiling or a sad human face according to whether the curve turns upwards or downwards. As an example of a less highly conventionalized icon, consider how an appropriate distribution of shades of white and grey may denote 'a tankard of cold, frothy beer' (see plate 2). The simplest form of advertising illustration is in fact the iconic image: a picture of the product against a neutral background.

In language, iconic signs (i.e. words) are relatively rare. In fact

Plate 2   Stella Artois (fragment)
Mayfair *August 1977*

it is a basic tenet of structural linguistics that typically there is no natural connection between a word and what it denotes; for instance there is no natural reason why the word 'horse' should denote a 'solid-hoofed herbivorous quadruped with flowing mane and tail' and not 'large bird of prey, with keen vision and powerful flight' (*COD*). Motivated linguistic signs — i.e. words which resemble what they denote — occur only in the relatively rare cases of onomatopoeia such as 'cuckoo', 'cock-a-doodle-do'.

Whereas the relation of similarity is of minor importance in the area of vocabulary, we find this relation playing an important role when we move to the use of language. In rhetoric, which is concerned with how to use language, the figure of metaphor can be defined by reference to the iconic relation: a word is replaced by another word which resembles it in meaning. Consider the following example:

> The forest, rooted, *tosses in her bonds*,
>   And *strains* against the cloud.
>   (Alice Meynell, 'The Rainy Summer')

The words which we have italicized are here used metaphorically: in a storm the forest moves as if it is chained to the ground and wants to pull itself loose. Note that metaphors do not occur only in poetry and 'rhetorical' prose, but also in everyday language. When we use such expressions as 'swallowing a book' or 'a loud shirt', we use metaphors.

In advertising language, metaphor is an extremely frequent device. Here, we shall mention only one example, namely Esso's famous 'put a tiger in your tank' campaign, where, of course, the word 'tiger' is used metaphorically (tiger = strength = Esso petrol).

An *index* is a sign which can be used to represent its object because it usually occurs in close association with it. In language there is an established rhetorical figure, metonymy,[4] which rests on the indexical relation. Standard examples of metonymy are 'the crown' for 'the king' and 'Whitehall' for 'the British Government'.

Indexical images are extremely frequent in advertising illustrations. Or rather, in their use of images many advertising illustrations try to establish an indexical relationship between the product and something else which is generally considered to carry favourable connotations. If the advert is successful, these connotations will then rub off on the product. Consider plate 3. apart from the statutory Government health warning, the advert consists solely of an illustration depicting a packet of cigarettes, a cup of coffee, and a glass of brandy placed on a red cloth. The verbal text, which is printed against the background of the illustration rather than in a separate box, is reduced to a minimum: we are informed only of the price of the product and of the fact that Silk Cut are Britain's biggest-selling low tar cigarettes. Thus the illustration is left to speak for itself, and the meaning is clear enough. Silk Cut cigarettes belong in the situation in which coffee and brandy also belong.

This attempt to establish an indexical relationship between a product and a desirable situation is extremely frequent in advertising images. The diamond ring advert which we considered briefly above, p. 35, builds on a firmly established convention, and the ring = love relationship actually recurs in several other examples. For instance

(21) A diamond engagement ring shows your love as nothing else can.

(Cosmopolitan, July 1977)

which is also part of an anchoring text of an advertisement for diamond rings showing both enlarged pictures of rings and a picture of a young couple. In fact the ring = love relationship is so firmly established that a ring alone can become a *symbol* of love by iconographic convention. But indexical relationships between love and commodities are also made use of in several other, less highly conventionalized cases: cosmetics, cigarettes, cars, alcoholic drinks, cookers, both gas and electric.

The tripartition into icon, index and symbol can be regarded as a division of signs in terms of decreasing degrees of naturalness: the icon is a sign whose connection with its object rests in some kind of similarity, the indexical relationship is a relation of contiguity, and finally the symbol is a sign where the connection between the sign and its object is based (more or less) purely on convention. The majority of linguistic signs (words) are non-motivated signs and, accordingly, symbols. Conversely, in the realm of images many apparently pure cases of symbols can be shown to have some 'natural' foundation: if we trace the history of a symbol back to its origin, we are likely to find some connection between the sign and its object. Thus a cross stands for 'faith' because Christ was

Plate 3   *Red Silk Cut*
Titbits *July 1977*

crucified; a dove is the symbol of 'peace' and 'hope' because doves are supposed to be very peaceful birds and because the return of the dove to Noah's Ark with an olive branch in its beak was a sign that the waters were receding; finally, a ring may be the symbol of 'love' because couples exchange rings.

The most clear-cut cases of visual symbols occur when a verbal metaphor mediates between the image and its object: a heart symbolizes 'love' because in the literary tradition that feeling is supposed to reside in the heart (see below, p. 79).

For obvious reasons, then, visual symbols are rare in advertising images: it takes a sustained advertising effort to establish a link between an arbitrary image and a product. Examples do exist, however. For instance, many makes of car have symbols which must be considered completely non-motivated (see plate 4). In other cases the product name is written in characteristic type, and the type itself comes to symbolize the product (e.g. Coca-Cola, Ford). But cases where a verbal metaphor mediates between symbol and product are

Plate 4   Car company symbols

more numerous, simply because the mediating verbal expression makes the link easier to establish. We have a fairly recent example of this in the case of Esso where a tiger has become a symbol of the product name after the 'put a tiger in your tank' campaign. The verbal metaphor behind the symbol in this case builds on the equation tiger = strength = Esso petrol. If the tiger stays in use after the slogan has been forgotten, the symbol will approach the status of a completely non-motivated symbol.

As another example of a verbally mediated symbol, consider how a particular breed of dog can come to stand for a particular make of shoes (Hush Puppies). Here the link between the symbol and the object is more obvious, because the mediating metaphor (puppies = softness = Hush Puppy shoes) occurs in the brand name itself.

Denotation and connotation

In our comments on the Carter—Thatcher photo (pp. 33-6; plate 1), we pointed out that as a means of communication pictures are much more ambiguous than language and that therefore they often have to be anchored by means of a verbal text. If pictures are so much more vague, and accordingly much less reliable, carriers of communication than language, one might well wonder why they are used at all. Why do we not rely exclusively on language? The answer, of course, lies in the very ambiguity of the image: what the image lacks in precision and clarity, it gains in richness of information. If, on the one hand, the image is less explicit than the verbal text, on the other it has the advantage of being able to communicate more things at one and the same time. Images, like poetry, thus call for interpretation, and in this way the addressee is forced to participate actively, if often subconsciously.

Let us take a closer look at the Carter—Thatcher photo. At one level it depicts a man and a woman. He is slightly taller than she. His right hand is raised in a gesture, his left hand seems to be in his pocket, his mouth is slightly open as if he is talking, his gaze seems to be fixed at a point that we cannot see. She is looking upwards at him, her head is slightly tilted, her mouth is closed and, to judge from the direction of her arms, she is holding her hands clasped in front of her. Barthes (1964) would say that the information which we have so far extracted from the photo is what is objectively there; anyone, according to Barthes, regardless of his cultural background, would be able to see this much. Barthes refers to the information which can be read out of a picture without recourse to cultural conventions as its *denotation*.[5]

If we go ahead with the analysis and ask ourselves what this particular configuration of two actors and their postures *vis-à-vis* one another 'means', we will have moved from the level of denotation to the level of *connotation*. It is not possible to give an exhaustive account of the connotations of an image, since the connotations evoked by a sign in an individual will depend on his entire previous experience, and consequently, the connotations of a given sign will vary slightly from person to person. On the other hand, in so far as members of a culture do in fact share experiences and expectations, the connotations of signs can in large measure be regarded as being common to all members of a culture.

The connotations of the Carter—Thatcher photo can be described in terms of three sets of opposing concepts:

1 *talking — listening*. Both the position of his right hand, which is frozen in the middle of a gesture, and his slightly open mouth, indicate that he is talking; whereas the tilt of her head and the direction of her gaze connote attentive listening.

2 *relaxed — concentrated*. His posture, with one hand gesticulating and, in particular, the other in his pocket, connotes self-confident relaxation. Whereas we are all aware of the connotative value of the hand-in-pocket posture, the connotation of the hands-clasped-in-front posture is not generally acknowledged to the same extent, but it nevertheless connotes deference/defensiveness/strain. To appreciate this, one only has to imagine the utter incongruity which would result if, for instance, she had held her hands clasped behind her.

3 *superior — inferior*. Together with the fact that he is shown as taller than she, the preceding observations all connote difference in status.

If it is true to say that the connotations of the same sign will vary between individuals, it is no less true that signs with the same denotations can have different connotations in different contexts. Consider two pictures of dogs: one the famous HMV dog listening to

'His Master's Voice' and the other a red silhouette of a dog against a white background on a gate. Whereas both images denote 'dog', the former connotes 'fidelity' and the latter 'beware of the dog'. Thus one may say that images denote their objects by virtue of their actual configuration of lines and colours, but that they can be *used* to connote various things according to the circumstances in which they are placed.

The relevance of the denotation—connotation distinction in language is well attested. Thus both 'horse' and 'steed' denote 'solid-hoofed herbivorous quadruped with flowing mane & tail' (*COD*), but they have different connotations because of the different contexts in which they are normally used. Leech (1966: 154) found that in advertising language the most frequent word for 'acquisition of product' was 'get', and not 'buy'. The reason for this is undoubtedly that 'buy' has some unpleasant connotations (money and the parting with it) which 'get' lacks (see further below pp. 67 ff.).

Visual emphasis

Above (pp. 21-3) we discussed how the positioning of the units of information in a text could be used so as to place varying degrees of prominence on them. In this section we shall discuss whether similar devices apply in the structuring of images. One important difference between verbal texts and images is that the verbal text, and its smallest unit, the sentence, has a beginning and an end, and can only be read by beginning at the beginning and ending at the end. Pictures, on the other hand, lack this temporal dimension: it is possible to survey a whole picture at once. However, something corresponding to a beginning and an end can be discovered in the case of images, quite probably because the way in which we scan a picture has been influenced by the way in which we read a page. When we read, the eye moves from the upper left corner of the page to the lower right corner, and the upper left—lower right diagonal is indeed an extremely important dimension in much painting, as well as in advertising lay-out.

To see how the diagonal is used to emphasize the most important parts of an advert, and to guide the eye towards the most important part of the message, consider plate 5. The illustration shows two women, one slightly older than the other. The older woman is standing behind the younger woman, who is sitting while she is applying

"I enjoy helping other women to look good."

And this is how I do it — I sell Avon. Women are busier than ever these days . . . often fitting in a job — at least part-time — with running a home and taking the children to and from school. They have little time to shop — and no time at all to spend making decisions at a crowded beauty counter.

That's where I come in. I bring the biggest beauty range in the world *right home to them*, and I help them to make the right choice of skin care products, make-up, perfumes and toiletries, often at very special prices.

In the peace and quiet of their own homes, they have *time* to try out the products, time to change their minds too — thanks to the Avon no-quibble guarantee.

You never looked so good.

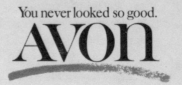

Plate 5   Avon
Cosmopolitan *April 1977*

some sort of eye make-up. Both women are staring at the younger women's reflection in the mirror which she is holding in her left hand. Note how the only clearly distinguishable parts of the photo (the heads of the two women and the younger woman's body and arms) occur along the upper left—lower right diagonal. This is achieved through the use of lighting and focus: the lower left corner, which is occupied by the older woman's body is shaded, and the visible part of the background in the upper right corner is out of focus, so that all we can see is that it is occupied by shelves with some indistinguishable objects on them. The headline occurring under the illustration ("'I enjoy helping other women to look good.'") is on the surface an example of relay: we immediately read it as being spoken by the older woman. But it also has an anchoring function: this picture illustrates the process of helping women to look good. And we now see a close correspondence between the headline and the prominent part of the illustration: the older woman is advising the younger woman on how to use the eye make-up. Note finally that if we follow the line running through the two women's heads and the younger woman's body, the eye is guided towards *the* most important part of the advert, the product name in the lower right corner of the page.

The upper left—lower right diagonal is by no means a universal organizing principle in advertising lay-out, but a trace of it recurs in the very large number of adverts where the product name, often accompanied by a picture of a sample of the product, occurs in the lower right corner of the advert (see, for instance, plates 8, 13, 28).

In some cases there are stylistic reasons for using another principle of organization. Plate 6 is the first page of a four-page advertisement for a series of medals issued on the occasion of Queen Elizabeth's silver jubilee. Note how this page is organized on a strictly symmetrical principle, 'befitting the true historic significance of the occasion' as the text has it.

We saw that one focal area of a page is the lower right corner. An equally prominent area centres around the point where the diagonal crosses the vertical median of the page. Lund (1947: 128) points out that the point upon which the eye tends to focus (the *optical centre*) is somewhat above the actual geometrical centre. If we return to the Avon advert (plate 5), we see that since the diagonal we have been discussing is a curve rather than a straight line, it

Plate 6   *The Kings and Queens Collection*
Reader's Digest *April 1977*

actually crosses the median in the optical centre, namely in the younger woman's right eye, so that the central area is occupied by her face. This accords well with the purpose of the advert, for although the text purports to be spoken by the older woman, the addressee is of course invited to imagine herself in the younger woman's role, being *helped* by Avon (remember that 'helper' is the typical actantial role of the product).

3

The Structure of an Advertisement

THE ADMAN'S TASK

The ultimate aim of all advertising is to sell the commodity, but in order to achieve this there are a few obstacles which the adman has to overcome. First of all, prospective buyers are likely to be reading the newspaper or magazine not because of its advertising material but because of its editorial material; moreover, round about half of the publication is likely to consist of adverts, all of them competing for the reader's attention. The first task of the adman, then, is to make sure that his advert is noticed. Once the reader's attention has been caught, the advert should also hold his attention and it should convince him that the subject of this particular advert is of interest to him. Furthermore, the advert has to convince the reader that the commodity will satisfy some need — or create a need which he has not felt before. Finally, it is not enough that the prospective customer should come to feel a need for the product in general; the advert must convince him that the particular brand advertised has some qualities which will make it superior to other similar brands. In addition, the ideal advert should be constructed in such a way that as much as possible of its message will get across even to the reader who merely notices it but decides not to read it.

Lund (1947: 83) summarizes the task of the adman as being to:

1 attract attention;
2 arouse interest;
3 stimulate desire;
4 create conviction;
5 get action.

We shall now investigate how these objectives are reflected in the structure of advertisements, but it must be pointed out from the start that it is quite rare to find an advert where it is possible to demonstrate a one-to-one relationship between the five steps set up by Lund and single elements in the advert. The normal thing is for two or more steps to be fused together.

TWO EXAMPLES

Dr White's

Consider the advertisement for Dr White's sanitary towels (plate 7). The advert consists of an *illustration* showing a woman, a man and a boy standing on a beach in the sunset. Printed on the background of the illustration is a *headline*, 'I came back', and, concentrated in one block in the lower left quarter of the advert, *body copy*; a *signature line* giving the name of the product, Dr White's; a *slogan*, 'Two kinds of comfort', and a picture of a package of the product on which the name of the product appears again.

Illustration   The three *actors* are standing close together, and are all touching each other; the boy is looking up at the man, who is looking at the woman, and she seems to be looking at both of them. The impression of closeness is further emphasized by the fact that their heads and the upper part of their bodies are encompassed by a line running from the boy's head, over the man's head, to the woman's head and through her neck and left hand (which is resting on the man's right arm), through his right hand and the boy's shoulder, and back to his head. They are obviously a family. They are slightly out of focus, so that their features are blurred. In this way they come to represent not individual persons or an individual family, but the universal family. For the same reason they are shown in the most universalized *setting* possible, a deserted beach.

The woman is leaning slightly towards her husband as if she has just walked in from the left of the picture (that is, we interpret the picture as a still taken out of a sequence of events — something has happened before, and something will follow; see Eco 1972: 276). She is clearly the most important of the actors and the point of

Plate 7   Dr White's
Woman *April 1977*

identification for readers; she is placed exactly in the middle of the picture, and her head is right in the optical centre of the picture. We are not in doubt that the headline is uttered by her (relay).

Headline   If we only had the headline and the illustration, we would take the two together as representing a situation where a woman returns to her family after an affair uttering the words, 'I came back.' But this is an advert for Dr White's. In the fictitious family situation of the illustration the woman is addressing her husband and the subject is their marriage; but in the advertising situation the real addressee is the reader, the real addresser is the advertiser, here speaking through the mouth of a 'secondary participant' (Leech 1966: 34), and the subject is the commodity. Along with the headline the most prominent items in the advert are the two occurrences of the brand name in the signature line and on the package. The headline thus becomes ambiguous: it may mean either 'I came back to my family' or 'I came back to my favourite brand of sanitary towels' or, rather, both at the same time (remember that ambiguity is a characteristic of the poetic function of language. In this way even the reader who only casts a casual glance at the advert will get the central message: 'returning to Dr White's after experiments with other forms of protection is like coming home to your family after an affair.' The technique employed is a double visual/verbal metaphor: Dr White's sanitary towels = safety = family.

Body copy   Throughout the body copy the woman remains the addresser, and accordingly ambiguity will arise whenever there can be doubt as to whether she is addressing the reader or the husband (or herself in a sort of inner monologue).

Although the copy is organized in one block, it clearly falls into three sections:

1 lines 1-5; in this section the poetic function of language is dominant.
2 lines 6-14; in this section the informational function is dominant.
3 lines 15-18; here the directive function is dominant.

As our main concern in this chapter is with the structure of the advert, we shall confine ourselves here to showing that the three sections have the functions indicated; hence we shall not go into any deeper discussion of the poeticisms employed in the first section or of the information value of the 'information' presented in the second section.

The first section continues the story which has been stated in the headline and illustration, and with the same ambiguity: is the 'softness and comfort' to which she came back the softness and comfort of the product or the softness and comfort of the family? Again, we are violating the nature of the poetic function of language by saying that it is an either/or; through the use of the metaphor it becomes possible to say something which could hardly be expressed in informational language without an obvious absurdity: Dr White's sanitary towels and the family are one and the same thing, and in this unity lies true 'softness and comfort'. In the second sentence of this section the ambiguity is resolved: 'I came back to Dr White's'. But the third sentence of the section again makes possible either, or both, interpretations: I 'went away' from Dr White's and/or from the family.

In the second section the following items of information are supplied: because of its cotton-wool content the product gives super-comfort and is softer; furthermore, the product is safer and more absorbent, and has a flush-away design. Note that what makes the function of language in this section informational is not the nature of the information given, which is fairly slight, but the way in which language is used: the poetic ambiguities which we noted in the headline and the first section of the copy are missing, the subject being clearly the product and the addressee being the reader. Further, in contrast to the first and third sections, the verbs in this section are only in the present tense ('gives', 'makes'), which is typical of descriptions of the permanent characteristics of things (e.g. 'Our house *has* four bedrooms').

In the first sentence of the third section we return to the narrative of the first section, but although the same scope for ambiguity arises, it is clear that 'the rest' must mean competing brands, and what she has come back to must be Dr White's. This sentence, then, is a recommendation of the product; that is, the function of language is expressive, and the justification for calling the function of this section directive lies in the last sentence of the section: 'Isn't it time you came back to Dr White's?' This is a negated interrogative sentence, but as is often the case with this sentence type, it is an exhortation to action rather than a question (cf. 'Isn't it time you began to do some work?'); that is, a directive speech act. Note also that this is the only time that the addressee, 'you', is mentioned.

Signature and slogan   We have already commented on the function of the signature line which is to establish the connection between brand name and the fictitious situation of the illustration and headline, thus getting as much as possible of the overall message across even to the most casual reader. To the reader who has read the whole advert, the slogan will appear simply as a repetition of the claim which is made for the product in the informational section — 'The super-comfort of their cotton-wool content' and 'a safer, more absorbent towel'. But for the reader who has skipped the body copy, the ambiguity which exists in this advert because of the tension between the situation depicted in the illustration and our knowledge of the fact that this is an advert, the slogan may well take a different meaning: Dr White's gives you 'two kinds of comfort', the comfort of a sanitary towel and the comfort and security of belonging in a family.

This is in many ways a classic advert which exemplifies clearly the adman's five tasks referred to at the beginning of this chapter. After the reader's attention has been caught ('attract attention') by the illustration and headline by means of an imaginary, universalized situation which can be expected to touch a chord ('arouse interest') in most potential readers (any married woman who has ever wished she could get away from it all),[1] the first, poetic section of the copy partly develops the home-coming theme, and partly tells the reader that the need for comfort and security which we all feel can be satisfied through using the product ('stimulate desire'). The second, informational section of the copy then makes the claims for the product, of double comfort ('create conviction'); and finally the last, directive, section appeals directly to the reader to go and buy the product ('get action').

Scottish Widows

In this advert (see plate 8) we find the same elements as in the Dr White's one: illustration — here divided into two — headline, body copy, signature and slogan.

The *illustrations* show a situation which will be familiar to all parents: being woken up early in the morning by a young child.

6 am. and Baby Bear has just found his porridge gone.

You know the feeling. You have one precious hour left before the day begins when this child arrives bright as a button to give you readings from her favourite book. And ask you questions to make sure you're paying attention. 'Now, who took Baby Bear's porridge?' And you hide your head under the pillow. But she finds it. 'Who took his porridge?' And you start to give in. 'Robin Hood?' 'No.' 'The taxman?' 'No.' And you're lost.

With children it isn't only nursery sagas that keep you awake. Or the things that go bump in the night. Sometimes it's just the responsibility. But you can share it. That's what life assurance is for. Take a Scottish Widows Family Income Policy for example. It will make

absolutely sure your children are well protected in the years they need it most. And help you sleep better.

At Scottish Widows that's what we believe life assurance is all about: helping you live your life to the full. Ask your broker about our approach. About our policies. About our record.

SCOTTISH WIDOWS
A better life assurance.

Plate 8   Scottish Widows
Reader's Digest *April 1977*

The familiarity of the situation is the main difference between this illustration and the Dr White's one, which attracted the potential reader's attention (in that case female) by showing a situation for which she might have felt a secret and unrealized desire. And this is the reason behind the different techniques employed. In the picture in the upper right corner of the Scottish Widows advert we see two recognizable (but not too individualized) persons — a little girl and her father — in a recognizable setting — a bedroom. (The setting is identified as a bedroom by means of some familiar *props*: a bed table with an alarm clock, and a chest of drawers with a lamp and some perfume flasks on it.) The girl is trying to wake up her father, who is desperately trying to stay asleep. In the smaller picture we see the same two persons now sitting together in bed, happily reading a fairy-tale book.

The *headline* in this case is not spoken by one of the actors (throughout the advert the reader, 'you', is addressed directly by the advertiser, 'we'), but is intended to help the reader identify the situation in the illustrations (anchorage). This is done by means of giving the time of the day and an allusion to a well-known fairy-tale.

The *body copy* is divided into three sections, here marked typographically, and again it is possible to characterize them according to their use of language as poetic, informational and directive.

The first section continues the thread from the headline and illustration, and at the same time the reader is directly invited to identify with the father in the illustration. The function of language is poetic not because of any ambiguity of roles — addresser, subject and addressee are unambiguously advertiser, parent—child relationship and reader — but because it attempts to generalize a particular experience: the feeling which we all know may not have any connection with Goldilocks, and the particular remarks which are passed between the father and his daughter are almost certain never to have been uttered by any of the readers of the advert. The generalization is achieved by means of the verb forms used. In a sense the section we are dealing with is a report of an event and, in this type of speech act, verbs are normally in the past tense, either simple or continuous ('My daughter came into the bedroom while I was still sleeping'), but here all the verbs in the report are in the present tense.

The second section moves from the event depicted in the illustrations and generalized in the first section towards a description (a speech act of the informational type) of the commodity, with the word 'nursery sagas' and the concept of being kept awake at night providing cohesion between the two sections. Here, too, most of the verbs are in the present tense, but in descriptions this is normal. There are four instances of the verb 'to be' in the simple present, all of which are descriptions of the 'eternal truth' type (compare 'it isn't only nursery sagas that keep you awake' and 'All that glitters is not gold'); there is one instance of the modal verb 'will' denoting what is 'typical or characteristic' (Leech 1971: 79) (compare [a life assurance] 'will make absolutely sure your children are well protected' and 'cork will float on water'). The sentence with 'can' is also a description, here denoting what is possible ('you *can* share it'). The only sentence in the section which does not exemplify an informational speech act is thus the imperative sentence ('Take a Scottish Widows Family Income Policy for example'). This type of imperative is used 'to further the development of the discussion or argument' (Huddleston 1971: 58), that is, a speech act of the interactional type. Its sole function is to make sure that the reader knows that what comes after is an exemplification of what has gone before.

The final section consists first of a declaration of the company's aims, which in the context of the situation functions as a commendation of the company, and, within the text, to provide the link between this and the preceding section. Secondly, the section contains an imperative ('Ask'), which is a direct invitation to action, i.e. a directive speech act.

Finally, the *signature* and *slogan* have the same function as in the Dr White's example: the reader who notices the advert but does not bother to read the copy will still get an idea of the basic message, that Scottish Widows has to do with a happy family life. Again we have a double metaphor: family life = happiness/security = Scottish Widows.

In the next three sections there follows a general survey of how the five requirements we mentioned at the beginning of this chapter are met in a large number of adverts. As requirements 1 and 2 (attention, interest) and 3 and 4 (desire, conviction) are often difficult to distinguish, and in practice are often collapsed, we shall treat each pair as one.

ATTENTION AND INTEREST

The reason why these two tasks are treated as one in many adverts is of course that one obvious way of catching the reader's attention is to show him (or her) that what the product has to offer is of interest to him/her. The elements of an advert responsible for this job are, as we have seen, the headline along with the illustration and slogan, if present.

The simplest way of arousing attention and creating interest is simply to place product's name alongside a picture of it. But since it takes extreme confidence in the selling power of one's product to ignore the more explicit appeals available, this approach is quite rare. On the other hand, the very simplicity of the technique can be its strength: if the advertiser is that confident in his product, it must be something very special. The advert reproduced in plate 3 is an example of the technique.

A far more common way of arousing interest, however, is to make some claim for the product in the headline/slogan. We have already seen examples of implicit claims (examples 12-13 on pp. 25-6), and we adduce just one more example:

(1a) How to offer your key people more life insurance for less.
(*US News & World Report*, June 1977)

which expects:

(1b) You can offer your key people more life insurance for less [money].

In a discussion of claims made in headlines, the type which most readily comes to mind is the *hyperbolic* claim. Familiar, and quite widely used, are the rather hackneyed 'now', 'new', 'improved', 'unique', 'Britain's best/biggest', etc., printed in distinctive type across the page or in exploding balloons (see plate 9):

(2) At last! An entirely NEW collection of beautiful underwear and lingerie
(*Cosmopolitan*, April 1977)

Note how 'At last' suggests that a new collection of underwear and lingerie is here available for the first time. Note also the

Plate 9 Babette
Cosmopolitan *April 1977*

exploding balloon in the upper left corner of the advert.

We have become so accustomed to hyperbolic statements that there is attention value in building up an expectation and then puncturing the hyperbole:

> (3) Thrilling conclusion of Buick Opel 5-Car Showdown.
>   Opel finishes . . .
>   [page turned]
>   uh . . . 2nd.
>
> (*Ms Magazine*, July 1977)

Another variant of the hyperbolic claim is the promise of free gifts or reduced prices. These have also become stock items in advertising language to such an extent that they can be played on consciously:

> (4) Banks don't give students free gifts for nothing.
> (*Sunday Times Magazine*, August 1977)

A safe way of creating attention and interest is to claim that the product will satisfy a need which already exists in the potential customer. We have seen two examples of this in the analyses of Dr White's, which played on the conflicting needs for excitement and security, and Scottish Widows, which played on the need for happiness. In both of these examples the appeal is to a social need, although one of them, Dr White's, satisfies an obvious material need.

Appealing to material needs is an obvious means by which advertisers seek to catch attention:

> (5) Stop itching fast.
> (*Reader's Digest*, August 1977)

Clearly, not every product can be expected to appeal to every reader of a magazine, and this fact is reflected in the headlines which directly single out the type of consumer to whom the product should be of interest. In the following example, the singling-out function is performed by an 'if' clause, whose purpose, to arouse and hold the reader's interest, is stated in so many words on the following imperative:

> (6) If your gums sometimes bleed when you clean your teeth, read on.
> (*Reader's Digest*, October 1977)

Two other sentence types in the headline or the opening line of the copy are often used with the purpose of identifying the potential reader and holding his attention, viz. questions and 'when' clauses (Leech 1966: 61):

(7) Have your legs ever felt so tired walking seemed like climbing?
                                            (*Ms Magazine*, May 1977)

    (8) When you've met your match
        Relax in a Radox bath
          (*News of the World*, September 1977)

But the simplest way of catching the attention of a limited section of the audience is to name them directly:

    (9) Denture wearers!
        (*News of the World*, September 1977)

This is often done by means of a noun-group beginning with 'for'. This type is particularly suitable for flattering the consumer ('for those who demand/expect perfection/the best'). The headline which singles out the interested segments of the audience can even be used in cases where practically all readers can be taken to belong to the category specified:

(10) Kotex Brevia are new. Small, slim, pantliners specially for
     every woman who's ever had to cope with vaginal discharge.
                                            (*Women*, August 1977)

It is remarkable that in the women's magazines studied, this type of headline, which singles out and to some extent individualizes the consumer, is quite frequent in the middle-class magazines (*Cosmopolitan*, *She*) but extremely rare in *Woman*, the majority of whose readers are working class. We shall return to this point in chapter 4, when we come to discuss how advertising approach varies with category of consumer.

    The types so far considered share the common feature that they try to catch the reader's attention by claiming that they have something to offer in which he/she should be interested. We shall now look at some examples where the attention-catching mechanism consists in an open attempt to arouse the reader's curiosity. The simplest type here consists in using the word 'secret' ('discover the secret of X'). In a more elaborate version the headline asks a question:

(11) How much do you see when you look at this painting?
(Sunday Times Magazine, August 1977)

Or it introduces a topic which is totally unexpected in the context:

(12) How the English brought peace to France.
(She, August 1977)

which is the headline of an advertisement for mustard. Finally, the surprise element may be of a purely linguistic nature, as when such rhetorical devices as *pun* (13), *metaphor* (14), *parallelism* (15) or *rhyme* and unconventional spelling (16) are used.

(13) Cutex Strongnail with nylon for long, strong, beautiful nails.
(She, August 1977)

Here the pun, which rests on the double meaning of 'nail', is both verbal and visual (see plate 10).

(14) *Angler's Mail* has got the nation hooked.
(Titbits, July 1977)

(15) Lookin' Foxy. Feelin' Fantastic.
(Ms Magazine, May 1977)

Note how the parallelism is reinforced by *alliteration*, (*f*oxy, *f*eelin' *f*antastic).

(16) The freezer-pleezers
(Woman, August 1977)

Finally and paradoxically, an advert may draw attention to itself by pretending that it is not an advert. Leech (1966: 99 ff.) refers to this phenomenon as *role borrowing*. The genres which are commonly used to lend interest to advertisements are the editorial article (usually with the warning 'advertisement' added, see plate 6), the comic strip (see plate 11) and the quiz:

(17) How much do you know about the real cost of electric central heating?
Test your knowledge in our Heating Plus Quiz
(News of the World, September 1977)

Role borrowing is a paradoxical phenomenon because these adverts try to make themselves conspicuous by resembling other genres in

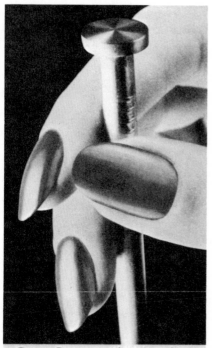

Cutex Strongnail with nylon for long, strong, beautiful nails.

Cutex Strongnail with nylon lets nails grow to their natural length by helping to prevent chipping and splitting.

Ten beautiful shades, including four new ones: Copper, Fire, Rose Quartz, Zircon. All with added nylon, to give you flexible, long-lasting colour–so as you care for your nails, your hands look beautiful too.

Cutex
Strongnail with nylon.

Plate 10   Cutex
She *August 1977*

Plate 11 Schloer
Sunday Times Magazine 31 July 1977

the publication, whereas the normal method is to make the advert stand out from the editorial material. The fact that the method is effective provides a nice illustration of the point made at the beginning of this chapter that the reader of a publication is more interested in the editorial material than in the advertisements.

DESIRE AND CONVICTION

In the analyses of Dr White's and Scottish Widows we saw how advertising can try to stimulate the reader's desire and create conviction in the quality of the particular product by further developing the idea from the headline/illustration/slogan which first caught his/her attention. In the two adverts in question, these two functions are performed by an opening poetic section and a following informational section in the body copy. This is very much the standard pattern, and very few advertisements refrain completely from using informational language in the body copy. The most notable exceptions come from three product groups — cigarettes (see plate 3), spirits (18) and cosmetics (19):

(18) He taught you to appreciate the finer things in life.
Make him glad he did.
[illustration: a bottle of whisky with a label saying 'To Dad' attached]
(*US News & World Report*, June 1977)

(19) Chique
Only some women have it.
(*Cosmopolitan*, July 1977)

To create real conviction in a product's superiority to competitors, an advertiser needs a 'Unique Selling Proposition' (USP), but, at our technological level, it is very rare for a product to boast a quality which is totally missing in competing products. For this reason the USPs which we are most likely to come across are essentially aesthetic (see pp. 8-9), such as the fact that a soap is transparent, or that a toothpaste has stripes. In the latter case the aesthetic product innovation is assisted by an aesthetic linguistic innovation:

(20) It tastes minty good.
(*Reader's Digest*, August 1977)

Even if an advertiser cannot claim that his product is unique, he can always describe how painstakingly the quality of each item has been checked. It is far more difficult to claim an advantage over competitors in the question of price. It is illegal to claim that a product is 'the lowest priced' of its kind unless one is able to substantiate the claim. But it *is* possible to say pretty much the same thing in different words. Since quality is a much more elusive concept than price, anyone can claim that his product is 'better value for money', or he can simply modify his claim with the word 'probably': 'X is probably the best buy/the lowest priced.'

The freedom with which advertisers can make claims about the quality of their products naturally makes these claims less credible. There are various ways to make up for this. One method is to have a celebrity recommend the product, whether directly or by association:

(21) [illustration: a racing car]
    [caption] Mario Andretti, in his Team Lotus Formula One race car.
    [headline] You, too, can depend on Valvoline.
    [body copy] Whenever and wherever Team Lotus races, this winner of 6 World Championships and 61 Grand Prix events depends on Valvoline® Racing Oil. Exclusively.
    You, too, can depend on Valvoline [...]
                    (*Reader's Digest*, August 1977)

Another method is to appeal to the authority of science or the medical profession. This can be done by using scientific-sounding abbreviations ('with NSM', 'with FG DC servo motor'), or by means of such standard claims as 'recommended by doctors', 'used in hospitals', 'the cleaner many dentists recommend'. Related to this is the technique of role borrowing which we discussed in the preceding section. An advert which pretends to be an editorial article is in a way parasitic upon the authority which a reader comes to associate with a publication he/she buys regularly. In an advert exemplifying role borrowing, the medical profession is again brought in, this time by giving the advert the form of a medical check list classifying types of headache and describing various treatments.

Finally, an advert can gain credibility by claiming that its product is compatible with generally recognized goals. The need to save energy, to fight pollution and to switch from non-renewable to renewable resources are recent examples of such goals, and, particularly in the US, these goals are now making their way into advertising. We see this tendency in the following example, which is an extract from a two-page prestige advert for a paper company:

(23) The wrong policies can make tree farming difficult and force the sale of forest land for other purposes. The right policies can assure continuation of America's forests — a renewable natural resource.

(Ms Magazine, May 1977)

ACTION

'Buy X!' is the most direct exhortation to action one can think of, but it is rare. In a count covering an issue of each of the ten publications on which this book is based, 'buy' in the imperative occurred only twice (see further below). We have already suggested (p. 44) that the tendency to avoid 'buy' might be put down to the unpleasant connotations of this verb. It is of course of vital importance to the adman that he should not appear to be imposing himself on his audience, for if the reader feels the advert to be too obtrusive, he/she is likely to react negatively to its message, or simply forget about it altogether. The adman is therefore confronted with a problem: on the one hand his advert should make people buy the product; on the other he must not say this in so many words lest they should take offence.

The majority of advertisements still fulfil the 'get action' requirement by using directive language of some sort in the concluding paragraph of the copy or in the slogan; but as many as 32 per cent (160 out of 498) in the sample refrain from using any direct exhortation to action. In advertisements which do call upon the audience to act, there are three methods used:

> imperative clause encouraging the audience to buy the product (32 per cent);
> other directive speech acts encouraging audience to buy the product (12 per cent);

directive speech acts inviting the reader to ask for a trial or for more information (23 per cent).

As mentioned, imperative clauses containing the word 'buy' are rare. In the sample, which comprises 179 imperative clauses in the concluding paragraph/slogan, it occurs only twice. The 20 most frequent verbs, accouting for 139 of the 179 cases, are the following:

try, ask for, get, take, let/send for, use, call/make, come on, hurry, come/see/give/remember/discover, serve/introduce/choose/look for

A number of these are obvious synonyms for 'buy' ('try', 'ask for', 'get', 'take', 'send for', 'use', 'choose', 'look for'), and others too, inserted in their contexts, turn out to mean little more than 'buy' ('make X your toothpaste', 'give him/her an X', 'discover the smoothness, etc. of X', 'introduce your family to X', 'serve X', 'let X solve your problems'). A smaller group does not ask the customer to buy the product, but tries to make sure that its name will be present in his/her mind in the buying situation: 'look for X at your dealer's', 'remember, there's only one X'; and the final group asks the customer to contact the dealer/agent with greater or lesser urgency: 'call/see your X agent', 'come to our showroom', 'come on/hurry, book now'. This final group is particularly frequent in advertisements for services such as insurance and travel, or for products in the more expensive range, such as cars.

In adverts using more cautious, indirect ways of calling to action, we find a variety of methods, ranging from openly directive language to language which can only be read as directive because of its context. The strongest of these methods is the negated interrogative which we noticed in Dr White's ('Isn't it time you came back to Dr White's?'). A slightly softer alternative form of this type is the 'Why not?' question ('Why not change to X?'). At the openly directive end of the scale we also find sentences with 'should' expressing admonition or advice (You should use X every morning), which is only just a shade softer than an imperative ('use X'). An even softer way of expressing advice is to leave out any mention of 'you' and only talk about the product: 'X is worth trying.' By virtue of the meaning of 'worth', this is obviously a piece of advice, i.e. a directive speech act, although it is expressed in a declarative sentence. In an example like the following on the other hand, it is only the context which indicates that the main clause should be read as a piece of advice:

(24a) for those who agree that additives are best left out, there's JOHNSON'S Baby Shampoo.

(*Cosmopolitan*, July 1977)

Note how the tone changes if we mention 'you' and use words or clause types normally associated with directive speech acts:

(24b) if you agree that additives are best left out,
$\left\{\begin{array}{l}\text{you should try JOHNSON'S Baby Shampoo.}\\\text{try JOHNSON'S Baby Shampoo.}\end{array}\right\}$

At the least openly persuasive end of the scale, we find sentences which, on the face of it, offer the customer advice on a product's use or availability rather than advise to buy it. The modal verbs 'can' and 'will' are characteristic of this type:

(25) you can use it at the table as well as in your cooking.

(*She*, August 1977)

(Compare this with 'you should use it' or 'use it'.)

(26a) You'll find [X] on all good cosmetic counters.

(*Cosmopolitan*, July 1977)

From one point of view, the 'you'll find' sentence is informational, but in fact it is of course equivalent to a directional speech act:

(26b) Look for/ask for [X] at all good cosmetic counters.

Again, it is the context which allows us to conclude that a sentence masquerading as information or advice is in fact an exhortation to action.

If it is considered too obtrusive to tell the consumer to go and buy the product, the advertiser can at least ask him/her to send for more information or to make a trial of the product. From the point of view of the advertiser, this has a number of advantages:

1 he gets direct feedback on the efficiency of his advertisement;
2 when the customer has contacted the advertiser, it is possible to follow up this response with a direct, personal address;

3 whereas it is vital for the survival of the advertiser that somebody should buy his products, most advertising represents the advertiser—customer relationship *as if* the advertiser is doing something for the customer. But when the advertiser is promising a brochure or a trial run, he is *in fact* offering to do something (although the cost of these services is of course included in the price of the product).

As for linguistic methods, there is very little to add to the points already made. The vast majority of advertisements using this less obtrusive technique ask the consumer to 'write/send/call' for more information, to 'fill in' and 'post' the cut-out coupon, or to 'contact your dealer/come along to our show-room for a trial run/a demonstration'. If it is deemed desirable to avoid imperative verbs, the direct exhortation to action can be passed off as advice: 'you can find out more about X by posting the coupon' and 'enquiries to'; or information: 'your dealer is always ready to fill you in on the whole picture/to show you our latest models/to give you a test drive'.

4

Strategies of Address: Sex and Class

AUDIENCE TARGETING

Consider the two adverts for Simplicity press-on towels from different women's magazines (plate 12). What is striking is their near-identity: they use the same format of picture narrative, beginning with long and medium shots of the protagonist, ending with a close-up of her smiling happily. Also, the verbal texts have many features in common: 'Everyone stayed later than I planned'/ 'we've stayed much later than I planned'; but, wearing Simplicity towels, 'I felt safe all day / so safe and secure'; both women conclude: 'I'm glad I switched.' Furthermore, the two advertisements contain precisely the same illustration of the product varieties and precisely the same slogan.

Yet the two adverts are also very different: the protagonists differ in terms of age, marital status and their main concerns in life. The older woman carries out the functions of a mother and wife; on the holiday boat-trip she tends their daughter and the food while her husband plays with their son; in short, she fits in with the traditional image of the family. The younger woman is just beginning to explore adult life as an individual ('moving into my first flat'), her main concern is to have fun with her friends; however, since the four young people are finally clearly divided into two couples, the scene suggests the younger woman's future transition to the role of the older woman in the other advert.

Not surprisingly, the first advert appears in *Woman's Own* (a magazine whose readership is very similar to that of *Woman*, cf. p. 11), while the second is found in *Cosmopolitan*. Taken together they demonstrate how adverts present a particular version

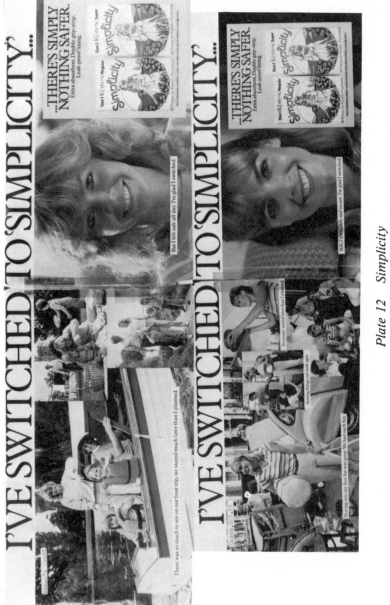

Plate 12 Simplicity

Woman's Own November 1981 ('boat trip') and Cosmopolitan October 1981 ('flat').
'Kotex', 'Simplicity', 'Brevia' are registered trademarks of Kimberly-Clark Corporation

of reality which is tailored to fit the presumed attitudes and values of the targeted audience. Nowadays most big advertising agencies employ both psychologists and sociologists who, equipped with the most recent readership surveys, try to determine which values and images are most likely to appeal to the audience of a given publication.

One of the assumptions underlying their strategic work is that advertisements should work on each reader's need for an identity, on the individual's need to expose himself/herself to lifestyles and values which confirm the validity of his/her own lifestyle and values, thereby making sense of the world and his/her place in it. What we are faced with here is a *signification process* whereby a certain commodity is made the expression of a certain content (the lifestyle and values).[1] Evidently, the ultimate objective of this signification process is to attach the desired identity to a specific commodity, so that the need for an identity is transformed into a need for the commodity.

Admen also have to take into account the fact that we filter the impressions bombarding us in order to ensure that only the most important ones have access to our consciousness. On the one hand, we weed out all irrelevant impressions; on the other hand, of all potentially relevant messages we are most likely to accept those which are in agreement with the views and values which we already have.

To the extent that these filters are different for men and women, middle class and working class, adults and children, and so on, as well as for the married and unmarried, for younger and older women, it is necessary for advertisers to allow for such varied receptivity and to tailor the presentation of their message accordingly.

The result of such strategic considerations may appear as the two different Simplicity adverts, aiming to persuade older, married women with children, and younger, unmarried ones, to 'switch to simplicity'.

MEN AND WOMEN

In its visual and verbal representation of the sexes, advertising comes to function as an ideological apparatus for the reproduction of our gender identities. Our respective identities as men and women are very important to us, especially to women for whom 'the signifier "woman" always signifies woman: we recognize ourselves in *any* representation of woman, however "original", because we are always already defined by our gender' (Winship 1980: 218 f.). Although many homosexuals and lesbians are beginning to assert their alternative sexual identities, it is still the case that individuals who violate the consensual norms of male and female behaviour frequently become victims of prejudice. Sometimes they may be ostracized from the social units to which they belong, whether family, peer group, or the community at large.

What constitutes a female and a male identity, according to advertising? To answer this question we may consider the commodity profile of three magazines, randomly selected from the range of publications studied in this book. The table below shows which commodities predominate in the advertisements covering more than half a page in *Cosmopolitan* (one copy), *Playboy* (one copy) and *Woman* (two copies). The percentages are based on a total of 241 adverts (87 from *Cosmopolitan*, 51 from *Woman*, 103 from *Playboy*):

Table 1   Commodity Profile of Three Magazines

	Percentage of adverts		
	Cosmopolitan	*Woman*	*Playboy*
Hygiene (shampoo, deodorant, sanitary towels, etc.)	26	10	3
Beauty (lotions, perfume, mascara, etc.)	39	18	1
Clothes (underwear, shoes, sweaters, jewellery, etc.)	7	12	14
Household implements (furniture, electric equipment, linen, etc.)	2	18	—
Food, detergents	5	31	—
Tobacco	6	8	15
Beer, spirits	3	—	25
Leisure (travel, books, etc.)	3	—	5
Technological toys (vehicles, photo, radio, etc.)	2	—	38
Employment	3	—	—
Investment insurance	3	2	—

We shall not comment exhaustively on the information provided by the table; we hope, however, that the reader will reflect on the percentages and on the possible communicative causes of their relative size. Why, for instance, do we find employment adverts in *Cosmopolitan*, but in neither *Woman* or *Playboy*? Or why do advertisers expect readers of *Woman* to spend more on clothes than the readers of *Cosmopolitan*?

For the purpose of studying strategies of address, it is sufficient to extract the general information on advertisers' expectations of male and female needs. Clearly, the products advertised in *Woman* emphasize a woman's role as a housewife, as someone who takes responsibility for the daily meals and the maintenance of the home. Even though the reader is still supposed to be attractive and to care how she looks, this is no longer seen to be her main concern. In *Cosmopolitan*, on the other hand, female beauty and appearance are uppermost, with suggestions as to how a woman can improve or preserve her assets, and the stress on her ability to attract man.

Men are also persuaded to acquire various products in order to improve their appearance. But, as we shall see, while the feminine ideal *rejects* the natural features of women's bodies — hair, eyes, skin, teeth, nails, lips, etc. — the beautification products offered to men (mainly clothes) are merely meant to *enhance* the natural features of men's bodies, not to transform them. Similarly, the figures for tobacco and spirits make it plain that the products offered to men are intended to function as outer attributes which create 'the real man'. The proper sphere for men is the throbbing life of society; as masters of technology they handle the serious and complicated business of life.

Our gender identities are also reproduced in individual adverts which reflect the fact that, in the popular consensus, man and woman are completely separate genders: if you are not a 'proper' man, it follows with inexorable logic that you are 'effeminate'; conversely, if you are not behaving 'like a woman', you will be stigmatized as 'mannish'. The possibility of a third or fourth type of 'natural' sexual identity is simply non-existent. Therefore, it becomes vital to stay on the right side of the gender demarcation line.

In *Cosmopolitan* (plate 13) we find an advert for Close-up toothpaste, asking: 'Your perfume turns him on. Will your breath turn him off?' This caption is accompanied by body copy and a

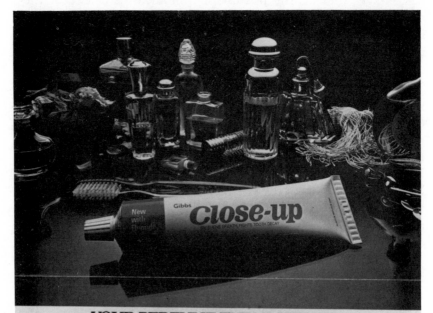

YOUR PERFUME TURNS HIM ON.
WILL YOUR BREATH TURN HIM OFF?

Close-up. Because life is full of them. Close-up. The strong, fresh breath toothpaste that gives you a cleaner-tasting

mouth and fresher breath.

Of course, it has fluoride. But Close-up has something else which makes it quite different from other toothpastes – a very special strong taste.

You can taste the freshness as soon as you brush your teeth.

So next time you pick up Close-up, don't just think of it as another fluoride toothpaste.

After all, you want to be as confident of your breath as you are of your perfume.

Close-up

BECAUSE LIFE IS FULL OF CLOSE-UPS

Plate 13   Close-up
Cosmopolitan *July 1977*

YOU KEEP YOUR BODY FRESH.
BUT IS YOUR BREATH A LITTLE STALE?

Close-up. Because life is full of them. Close-up. The strong, fresh breath toothpaste that gives you a cleaner-tasting

mouth and fresher breath.

Of course, it has fluoride. But Close-up has something else which makes it quite different from other toothpastes – a very special strong taste.

You can taste the freshness as soon as you brush your teeth.

So next time you pick up Close-up, don't just think of it as another fluoride toothpaste.

After all, you want to be as confident of your breath as you are of your body.

BECAUSE LIFE IS FULL OF CLOSE-UPS

Plate 14   Close-up
Sunday Times Magazine *July 1977*

picture of the tube and toothbrush lying on a woman's dressing table. A very similar advert is found in the *Sunday Times Magazine* (plate 14), picturing a man's dressing table and with near-identical body copy; the headline, however, asks: 'You keep your body fresh. But is your breath a little stale?' Why do the adverts for men find it necessary to vary the message in this way?

Let us first have a look at the similarities. In both adverts the hygienic use-value of toothpaste is absent, in fact as absent as soap is from the pictures which are dominated by beauty products. The aesthetic use-value dominates, making Close-up contribute to the no-flaw surface, always ready to be appraised, not risking to be weighed and found wanting — 'Because life is full of them [close-ups].' Also, in both adverts the absence of people and the photographic illusion which places the readers in front of the dressing table make it possible for them to insert themselves and to identify with the absent person.

The *Sunday Times Magazine* advert is addressed to a more mixed audience; for instance there are no gender-specific pronouns in the caption. However, the objects represented in the picture will appeal more to men, since they belong to a man's dressing table. Together with the *Cosmopolitan* advert, which clearly appeals to women only, this one says a lot about masculinity and male self-perception in the late 1970s: men do use various fragrances, so why can't the *Cosmopolitan* headline, with the proper change of pronoun, function with the *Sunday Times Magazine* picture?

The answer lies in the word 'perfume'. Twenty-five years ago men couldn't use fragrances without being branded as homosexuals. The first attempts by the cosmetics industry to expand sales to men consequently had to dress up fragrances as health products such as medicated hair lotion and after-shave lotion. Simultaneously, advertising campaigns were launched with the purpose of establishing a connection between certain smells and a brutish masculinity, trying to effect a mental redefinition of masculinity. These campaigns have been so successful that most men will now smear their faces and bodies with fragrances before going out to a restaurant or disco: 'Well placed, it's your most effective weapon. Racquet Club. Grooming gear for men' (*Penthouse*, September 1980). The whole thing is surrounded by self-delusion, because the fragrances are called 'deodorant', 'after-shave', and so on, never 'perfume'.

So today the actual application of fragrances displays little variation for males and females, but in their self-perception an important symbolic difference remains: men have not yet become women, the sexual barrier is intact.

ADDRESSING WOMEN

The ideal of domesticity

Traditionally, advertisements have shown women as mothers and wives, thereby upholding a feminine ideal of domesticity. This image still appears, but more rarely, as increasing numbers of women come to see themselves as more than guardians of the family and the home. A soft drink advert pictures a children's birthday garden party, the happy kids are standing around the garden sprinkler, one of them next to a super 'mom kids depend on to make days fun. That's a mom who depends on Kool-Aid.'

Another example is found in an advert for Crosby Kitchens (*Good Housekeeping*, April 1982, showing a relaxed housewife in a modern slightly rustic kitchen taking a break from her domestic duties and talking to her roguish eight-year-old daughter. The body copy assures us of the use-value quality of Crosby kitchens: 'They take the knocks and spills of family life — and still look good.' However, the caption promises a lot more than durability and efficiency: 'Crosby Kitchens are the ♡ of a good home;' the emotional value is reinforced by the connotations of the picture, and spelled out by the text printed on the woman's apron: 'Home is where the ♡ is.'

'Happy family' adverts like Kool-Aid, Crosby Kitchens and Simplicity all imply that if the female reader's everyday life isn't as happy and harmonious as that portrayed in the advert, the short-comings are in some way due to her inadequacy in fulfilling the functions required of a good wife and mother. The problems of the family, frequently socially determined, are thus individualized, and incipient despair is converted into a consumption-directed effort, which is allegedly capable of reinstating the agreement between the ideal image and experienced life.

Some adverts remind housewives of their duties in quite plain words. A Radox Herbal Bath advert (*Woman's Own*, October 1978) pictures a worn-out woman surrounded by toys, promising that 'We could make you a joy to come home to.' In other words, it suggests that a housewife has an obligation to cheer up her husband when he gets back from work, by making herself as appealing as possible: 'Your husband will be home in twenty minutes. Do you really feel up to giving him a bright and lively welcome. A Radox bath could make all the difference.' Apparently, a woman without a paid job has no right to be tired and admit that she's exhausted.

Still, the image of domesticity doesn't have the persuasive effect it once had, for instance in the mid-1950s, when OXO meat cubes were sold because of the 'man-appeal' of housewives using OXO cubes in stews and pies: 'Katie, the eager young bride, existed only to serve Philip [. . .] his delicious OXO stews' (Faulder 1977: 41). Then the promise of 'man-appeal' was taken seriously because every woman wanted to be 'a wife who always waited for her husband and rushed to serve him the moment he arrived home' (Faulder 1977: 42).

In OXO campaigns of the mid-1970s the 'man-appeal' still was used. OXO now has 'twice the man-appeal' (*Woman*, October 1977) because its flavour is now bigger, 'an even beefier, more OXO-y taste'. This claim that the beef strength of a cube and its man-appeal are directly proportional, together with the picture of *two* satisfied 'husbands', clearly show that the 'man-appeal' should not be taken seriously. By making fun of former advertising campaigns which exploited the domestic image, this advert slightly ridicules the associative chain connecting OXO and man-appeal: 'Despite breaking through the cliché [. . .] on one level, at another the ad uses it fully' (Williamson 1978: 34).

Instead of emphasizing an idyllic image of domesticity, modern advertising will find a broader perspective in concentrating on the problems faced by the majority of women today, who have paid full- or part-time work while also being in charge of the domestic chores. Thus an advert for an electric freezer clearly assumes that the woman addressed is responsible for the provision of food: she is aware of the movement of food prices with inflation and the seasons, the advantages of 'buying in bulk' or baking 'more than you need and freeze the rest to eat later on'. The advert also allows for the possibility that she is employed outside the home: 'If you're working all day, with no time to shop, a fridge-freezer can be a real life-saver!' It is in this context that the first promise of the advert should be seen: 'A fridge-freezer gives you the best of both worlds.' Instead of feeling inadequate as a housewife while she is at work, and rushing from shop to shop desperately after work, she will be able to have, thanks to a fridge-freezer, 'the best of both worlds': that of traditional female responsibilities and that of paid work.

This and several other adverts thus truthfully reflect the fact that although women have become accepted on the labour market, the bulk of the household chores are still regarded as their responsibility. And the suggestion that the solution to the problems created by this double role lies in the consumption of commodities is of course totally consistent with the role of advertising (see also below p. 131).

The strait-jacket of the beauty ideal

The dominant image of femininity in advertising today is that of the beauty and fashion ideal. The transition from the domestic woman to the glamorous woman is aptly reflected in the following: 'Don't let motherhood spoil your bustline . . . Thousands of women have used Aqua-maid to keep their bustlines firm and youthful — why don't you join them? (*Cosmopolitan*, July 1977). According to advertising, female priorities seem to have switched from motherhood and childcare to the maintenance of their physical appearance.

This beauty and fashion ideal has become the new strait-jacket of femininity, requiring women to compete through their appearance for the attention of their husbands, lovers, bosses and any other specimen of the male sex they happen to encounter. According to Berger (1972: 47) this ideal is a passive one, controlled by the Male Eye:

Men act and *women appear*. Men look at women. Women watch themselves being looked at. This determines not only most relations between men and women but also the relation of women to themselves. The surveyor of woman in herself is male: the surveyed female. Thus she turns herself into an object — and most particularly an object of vision: a sight.

This needs some elaboration. Although the ideal of woman is ultimately a passive one, 'today's woman' as portrayed by advertising is quite active. In most cases, however, her activity consists in transforming herself into a passive object awaiting the man's initiative. For instance, a nail cream advertisement requires the woman to engage in a quite laborious beautification process; afterwards she can lean back and 'Let L'Érin Color Glaze do the talking' (*Cosmopolitan*, American edn, March 1982). In another advert, a woman proudly says: 'When I walk down the street I get whistled at now' (*Woman*, August 1977).

Although men are the ultimate arbiters of the beauty contest between women, some women take it upon themselves to enforce the beauty ideal, using 'the ugly face of gossip' as their chief weapon. In this way the Male Eye determines 'also the relation of women to themselves' (Berger 1972). The TAO advert for removing 'unwanted' hair by electrolysis starts out by asking whether 'other people talk about the hair you don't want to talk about' (plate 15). In the accompanying picture 'you' (the woman averting her face) is excluded from the confidence shared by the 'other people' (the two women to the right), who with mixed compassion and malice are talking about 'your' physical and social handicap — which 'you' yourself recognize as a handicap and therefore 'don't want to talk about'. The advert thus takes for granted a universally shared repugnance for 'unwanted' hair, because excess body and facial hair places a woman on the wrong side of the gender demarcation line. In order to win back the confidence of her two friends, it is not necessary for the woman to adapt herself to their attitudes and norms, all she has to do is to implement the views she already shares with them. This is where the services offered by TAO become indispensable.

This advert exploits the negative side of gossiping (for the positive side, see pp. 93 ff.): women's malignant talk behind the backs of friends and neighbours which to some extent ostracizes them from the community. Adverts wield a powerful weapon when they suggest that certain physical features (and natural ones at that!) are the subject of scandalmongering, and victimize the women who don't live up to such definitions of femininity.

In order to explore this ideal further, consider the advert formerly used for Anne French deep cleansing milk, as it appeared in *Cosmopolitan* in July 1977 (plate 16): the whole tone of it shows that it is written with some self-irony, for instance the name (Robert Newford) of the filmstar interviewed by the young reporter

Do other people talk about the hair you don't want to talk about?

How would you like to remove it forever? Talk to Tao. For the following reasons.

● Unlike some people today, Tao use a tried, tested, and proven method of removing unwanted hair. For over 40 years we've brought happiness to thousands of women.

● Tao treatment is recommended by doctors, hospitals and beauty consultants. ● Tao offers real value for money. Just compare our cost with that of other companies. Just add up how much it costs you in creams etc. over the years.

● Tao treatment gives a permanent answer to the problem of unwanted hair by a course of Electrolysis.

●Initial consultation is free, and without any obligation. ●There are 33 Tao Clinics throughout the country. There's one near you.
So talk to Tao. And stop people talking about that unwanted hair forever.

153 Brompton Road, London, S.W.3. (7 DOORS PAST HARRODS)

Tel: 589 4847, 589 5425, 589 7281 & 589 9055

THE TAO CLINIC (BRANCHES) LTD. *at* **Aberdeen** *(Tel: 56601).* **Birkenhead** *(Tel: 647 7472).* **Birmingham** *(Tel: 643 5471).* **Bournemouth** *(Tel: 22427).* **Brighton** *(Tel: 25436).* **Bristol** *(Tel: 28482).* **Cambridge** *(Tel: 62848).* **Cardiff** *(Tel: 26276).* **Carlisle** *(Tel: 27840).* **Chester** *(Tel: 20612).* **Edinburgh** *(Tel: 225 2642).* **Exeter** *(Tel: 73860).* **Falmouth** *(Tel: 313984).* **Glasgow** *(Tel: 332 8866).* **Hull** *(Tel: 23746).* **Leeds** *(Tel: 453237).* **Leicester** *(Tel: 544455).* **Liverpool** *(Tel: 709 5305).* **Manchester** *(Tel: 832 5466).* **Newcastle-on-Tyne** *(Tel: 21852).* **Norwich** *(Tel: 24446).* **Nottingham** *(Tel: 48494).* **Oxford** *(Tel: 49347).* **Penzance** *(Tel: 2110).* **Plymouth** *(Tel: 266450).* **Preston** *(Tel: 59046).* **Redruth** *(Tel: 21560 or 215394).* **St. Austell** *(Tel: 4566).* **Sheffield** *(Tel: 78481).* **Southampton** *(Tel: 23181).* **Swansea** *(Tel: 55316).* **Truro** *(Tel: 3946). And Toronto, Canada.*

Plate 15   TAO
Cosmopolitan *July 1977*

protagonist, Felicity Brown, is humorously distorted, but easily recognizable as that of a well-known Hollywood figure. The writer is well aware that people don't believe the exaggerated claims of advertising, and by choosing this hyper-clichéd format, he exploits their disbelief by pretending to share it. At the same time, however, he manages to invoke the myths and dreams of the reader's sub-conscious, so that in spite of their being made fun of, these dreams can be exploited to the full. Like Felicity Brown, the female reader is dreaming: 'one day it would happen. Her big chance. And she'd be ready for it. . . One day it did.' And like Felicity, she cannot afford to dismiss any accessory which may help her obtain the highest rewards for today's woman: the appreciation of an attractive, prestigious man *and* a scoop in her job; in other words, success in terms of traditional femininity and liberated femininity, beauty and work — the latter dependent on the former.

In all its humorous blatantness, then, this advert exposes the basic rationale of female beautification: in order to become happy (cf. Felicity/felicity) and successful a woman has to be beautiful. Until the moment of happiness and success occurs, she has to live sus-pended in expectations of a marvellous future, ceaselessly and carefully applying the cosmetics prescribed by advertising, remembering that even the most 'ordinary kind of day' may prove to be the turning point of her life. For some, it may even be necessary to undergo cosmetic surgery if they don't 'reflect the right image' (*Cosmopolitan*, July 1977).

Quite a few cosmetic adverts openly admit that the beauty ideal is based on deceit. An advert for Max Factor foundations (plate 17) uses the mirror technique, creating the illusion of looking at a perfect version of yourself as you may become by using the product; this effect is achieved by picturing the life-size face of a model, accom-panied by the caption 'Is her skin really this beautiful?' Some adverts might have chosen to answer in the affirmative, since that would provide a basis for offering the consumer the means to achieve the perfect skin. This one, however, adopts the honest approach: 'Not without a little help, it isn't.' In other words, Max Factor invites you to a little deceit, which the slogan elegantly connects with a self-evident feminine ideal: 'Don't you love being a woman? Max Factor.' The form of the question invites a 'Yes', which is replaced by 'Max Factor', implying that 'Yes' *means* 'Max Factor'.

scoop!

Felicity Brown was a junior reporter on a local newspaper. It was mostly routine. Flower shows.... Bazaars.... Protest Meetings. But Felicity dreamed. One day it would happen. Her big chance. And she'd be ready for it....

One day it did. An ordinary kind of day, it seemed.

She was sitting at her desk, correcting some proofs. It was raining. She was bored.

Then the editor appeared. Shouting through the office. "Get a reporter down to the Metropole fast. Robert Newford is staying there."

The news editor looked at her. He grinned. "It's your day," he said to her. "It'll have to be Felicity," he said to the editor. "There's no-one else here." "He grinned. "It'll have to be Felicity," he said to the editor. "There's no-one else here."

The room spun briefly. Her heart did funny things. It can't be true, she thought, I must be dreaming. But it was and she wasn't.

The editor looked anxious. "Can you cope?" he said.

Felicity's nerve steadied. "I can cope" she said.

The interview was easy. He was charming, relaxed, funny. He even talked slowly; she got down every word. Then at the end he grinned at her. "How nice," he said,

to meet a pretty young reporter for a change." She took care of her skin with Anne French. It kept it super-clean, super clear. So she always looked wonderful. And Robert Newford wasn't the only one who noticed ...

ANNE FRENCH
DEEP CLEANSING MILK

ROBERT NEWFO[RD]
TALKS TO
FELICITY B[...]

Plate 16   Anne French
Cosmopolitan *July 1977*

Is her skin really this beautiful?

Not without a little help, it isn't.

Max Factor Foundations are too sheer, too light, to be seen. But the results can't be missed. Choose from: Velvet Balanced Make-up – a pH balanced, oil-free liquid to maintain your skin's natural acid balance.

Velvet Touch. A gossamer light, basic foundation to give your skin a fresh radiant look.

Ultra Moist. A creamy, richly moisturised foundation that's especially kind to drier skins.

Use one of these foundations from Max Factor and they could be asking it of you. Is her skin really that beautiful?

Foundations from

DON'T YOU LOVE BEING A WOMAN? MAX FACTOR.

Plate 17   Max Factor
Cosmopolitan *October 1981*

An unquestionable standard of beauty also forms the starting point for an advert for mascara. If your eyelashes are not ideally dark and long, you must do something about it; the language of advertising doesn't give you the chance to decide *whether* you want to emulate the ideal, only *how* to become a perfect version of yourself: 'You won't believe your eyelashes. Even the shortest, lightest lashes can be really longer, darker in seconds' (*Cosmopolitan*, July 1977). This is even more plain in another advert whose caption claims that 'Our moisturiser is better than your moisturiser' (*Cosmopolitan*, July 1977); it displays such a degree of infallibility that it will be difficult for the woman who doesn't use a moisturiser not to feel slightly abnormal.

The last sentence of the Max Factor advert mentioned above promises that if the reader uses a Max Factor foundation 'they could be asking it of you. Is her skin really that beautiful?' Again, the answer would be no, but the interesting thing about this sentence is that it points to the deliberate cultivation of envy in adverts: one firm sells make-up 'to keep you looking enviably calm' (*She*, August 1977), another will 'help you obtain naturally, the best, most enviable suntan' (*Cosmopolitan*, July 1977). This exploitation of envy is a general feature of advertising:

Publicity is always about the future buyer. It offers him an image of himself made glamorous by the product or opportunity it is trying to sell. The image then makes him envious of himself as he might be. Yet what makes this self-which-he-might-be enviable? The envy of others.

(Berger 1972: 132).

Again, this may have psychological consequences for the individual:

Being envied is a solitary form of reassurance. It depends precisely upon not sharing your experience with those who envy you. You are observed with interest but you do not observe with interest — if you do, you will become less enviable.

(Berger 1972: 133)

Why do women accept advertising's ideal of femininity?

As we have shown in the previous section, advertising presents a feminine beauty ideal which doesn't recognize beauty as a property resulting from natural characteristics. No woman can attain the ideal without purchasing and applying a number of manufactured cosmetics; depending on her natural predispositions she will have to apply a smaller or larger selection, but all women have to use some: 'Even a perfect skin needs constant and regular beauty care' (*Cosmopolitan*, July 1977).

Our argument is not that women should never paint their eyes, cheeks or lips, never colour their hair, never use fragrances, and so on. What we *are* saying is that women *and* men should be able to experiment creatively with body aesthetics, having in mind objectives other than the attraction of the opposite sex. The beauty ideal presented by advertising stands in the way of any attempt to create a more open-minded ideal, especially one which requires fewer commodities for its maintenance.

So why do women accept an ideal of femininity which allows no excess body or facial hair, no spots on the skin, requires obligatory long eyelashes, and so on?

The first answer is: they don't. We have tried to show that the women portrayed in adverts are passive, waiting for men to take the initiative. Yet a survey of the conscious attitudes of *Cosmopolitan* readers shows that around 70 per cent of the respondents 'said they were willing to make the first move towards someone they fancied' (Jones, 1982b). Similarly, in a portrait of the typical *Cosmopolitan* reader, Jones (1982a) thinks that she 'wants good sex for her own pleasure and can provide the good life for herself...Sex? Yes. Sex object? Never!' Although the editorial content of *Cosmopolitan* aims to reflect a more whole, self-sufficient image of woman, the fact is that advertisers still seem to believe that women will succumb to an ideal which contradicts their consciously held views on 'the new woman'.

The second answer is that women don't necessarily regard the present ideal as an expression of female subjection to the norms of a patriarchal society: *Cosmopolitan* readers don't want to live 'entirely through *him*. That means you're going to make the most of yourself — your body, your face, your clothes, your hair, your job and your mind' (Jones, 1982a). According to this view, then, a woman makes herself beautiful for her own sake, not to please men. Nevertheless, when women find it 'permissible and even desirable...to want success" (ibid.), don't they have to follow 'the rules of the game' of a male-dominated society?

The third and most important answer seems to be that we haven't distanced ourselves from our deep-rooted values: 'Liberation [is] just a word, and reality lag[s] a long way behind' (ibid.). Even an advert addressing women as job-seekers plays upon the consensus that a woman's principal task is to find a man — responsibility and challenge are offered, of course, but we soon discover that Christine has not only made a large number of friends in her new job, she has found a fiancé too.

Most adult women have been brought up to accept the subservient woman as the natural woman, and it can be argued that many of the personal and marital problems facing women may seem to them to be caused by their reluctance to live up to the traditional norms of feminine behaviour. The traditional images of femininity may then subconsciously acquire the status of a peaceful haven where roles were well defined and identity conflicts non-existent.

Being in the dream business, advertising is far too smart to present a balanced and accurate view of society as it is. As long as most women still see themselves as housewives, advertising will continue to address them as such, in spite of statistics proving that more than sixty per cent of married women are wage-earners. The best evidence that women do still perceive themselves in terms of traditional images is the fact that they don't use the power they have 'to cause the downfall of offensive adverts: we can choose not to buy the products they sell' (Mower, 1981). By presenting an overall image of subservient femininity, adverts can be said to exploit the nostalgic longing of women (and men) towards the days when life seemed more straightforward.

The independent woman

[The Cosmopolitan reader] is not swallowing the male work ethic hook, line and sinker [...] We've side-stepped elegantly past the pit that said that if women wanted to enter a man's world they must act more like men. Instead, we're bringing in fresh, female and guaranteed unsettling views of our own.

(Jones, 1982a)

This may be so in the editorial third of the pages of *Cosmopolitan*, but in the two-thirds taken up by advertising, the economically independent, working woman is conspicuous by her almost total absence, even though women hold over forty per cent of the total jobs in Britain (ibid.). And in the few cases where she is portrayed in adverts, her job is seen to belong to the more prestigious end of the occupations.

An advert for the Halifax Building Society (*Cosmopolitan*, July 1977) pictures a woman on the job, a busy career woman, probably a manager in fashion clothes with a colourful life. A Tampax advert (plate 18) shows a woman at work in what is probably a busy art gallery where she has 'important decisions' to make. The criteria which give her success in her job are the same criteria which she applies to period protection aids: 'I trust the facts. But first I check them out. It's the only way to feel confident when you're working against time [. . .] And once you've checked the facts, you'll trust Tampax tampons.'

Neither in the pictures nor in the texts are there any indications of a refusal to comply with a rational, competitive male work ethic. Apparently, in its portrayal of the work sphere, advertising has no room for the more emotional, co-operative ethic which many women would like to see permeate all spheres of life.

The ideal of masculinity

Men are rarely present in the adverts directed at women. But when they are, they are usually a kinder, more friendly type, more understanding, less macho than the men portrayed in adverts directed at a male audience. The family father of some adverts (e.g. plate 12) is dominant in an inconspicuous and friendly way; the men in a French Almond advert (*Cosmopolitan*, July 1977) are the moderately tough-guy type; and the building society employee is the helpful adviser, initiating the woman into the jungle of the financial world.

It is also in women's adverts that we meet 'the new man', for instance in *Cosmopolitan*, whose editorial pages have 'been there with support and encouragement as men have started to come out of the closet and admitted to having emotions and fears of their own' (Jones 1982a). But the only example of the 'new man' which we found is in an advert for British Gas (plate 19) where a man and a woman are pictured in their kitchen, both smiling, the man grating cheese. This man is not your traditional tough guy or career

"I trust the facts"

"But first I check them out. It's the only way to feel confident when you're working against time and have important decisions to make!"

And once you've checked the facts, you'll trust Tampax tampons. To begin with, more women use them than all other tampons combined. That's because they trust the protection Tampax tampons give. More than sufficient dependable protection for their normal needs.

When a tampon is in use,

embarrassing odour does not form.

There are also no unpleasant disposal problems with Tampax tampons. Both the tampon and its container-applicator are flushable and biodegradable. This makes good sense ecologically.

In spite of all these advantages Tampax tampons are still more economical than most other tampons. They come in packets of 10 and 40. The 40's in particular make Tampax tampons a really economical buy. A lot more protection for your money.

These are some of the reasons millions of women use Tampax tampons. Once you know the facts, they will be your choice, too.

MADE ONLY BY TAMPAX LIMITED, HAVANT, HAMPSHIRE

The internal protection more women trust

Plate 18   Tampax
Cosmopolitan *July 1977*

Plate 19   *British Gas*
Cosmopolitan July 1977

man: he is a gentle intellectual who takes part in the cooking, not just as a 'help' to his wife, but as a natural male function when both husband and wife work outside the home: 'Margaret is a geophysicist. . . Vance is an historian of science.'

Still, although she is a scientist, when it comes to the cooking of meals, Vance's comments are of a more technical type while Margaret is practical enough to be wearing an apron and seems to be responsible for the more menial duties in connection with cooking: 'I've not had to really clean the oven in the 10 months we've had it.' And while she describes the ease with which she cooks 'a steak and kidney pudding at the top and baked apples underneath', he describes how the simmer control is particularly important for his leisure activity of brewing beer.

The image of sex roles in this advert is therefore quite emancipated as adverts go, but still it operates within a world where alternatives to the nuclear family are inconceivable.

The alternative face of 'gossip'

In a previous section we saw how adverts exploit the reprehensible face of gossip which is the only visible one in a male-dominated society: the TAO advert victimized women with 'unwanted' hair by subjecting them to gossip.

Most people probably think of gossip as a female domain. Originally, however, gossip was not limited to women. Etymologically rooted in the Old English 'god sib', the word meant a sponsor at a baptism, usually a close relative. Later it came to mean a family acquaintance, still without sex-specific reference. Not until the seventeenth century is the word exclusively applied to women, who were active in connection with childbirths: 'Since men were not allowed to attend birth, the people at a home delivery were women [. . .] a home delivery was a general coming-together of all the women of the community' (Rysman 1977: 178). It is only after 'gossip' is applied to a gathering of women, closed to men, that it develops a verb form and acquires the negative undertone. This can be seen to reflect the insecurity of the excluded men towards the unity and confidence shared by the women: men were afraid of women gossiping behind their backs, because 'even when used in a derogatory manner the meaning of the term gossip has retained its implications of solidarity (ibid.).

The alternative face of gossip thus stands for an exclusive female relationship in a male world, a relationship which enables women to exchange experiences, complaints, secrets and mutual help without male interference, a tradition of sisterhood before feminism.

Many of the adverts which address women appropriate this female form of solidarity, exploiting it with the objective of making women comply with patriarchal definitions of femininity. These parasitical adverts, which rely on a female protagonist and/or a personal testimony can be divided into four subtypes depending on the presence of a female protagonist with or without a 'helper', and the function and direction of the personal testimony:

(a) *The full structure*   In a cartoon advert for Stop'n grow (*Jackie*), we meet an ordinary young girl who was 'really winning with Steve — and not just at cards. Then he noticed my bitten-down nails.' Fortunately, Susie drops in, and three weeks later: 'Susie was right! *Stop'n grow* is great. No more hand-hiding for me. No more bitten nails. I'm too busy holding hands.'

This advert establishes a full 'gossip'-relation between three women: Susie assists her friend-in-distress, who by describing the course of events assists the reader as a potential friend-in-distress. The same pattern is found in a non-cartoon advert for Soft and Gentle Anti-perspirant (plate 20) where a job interview ends in success 'thanks to my clever old flatmate and her Soft and Gentle'. The communicative relationship between protagonist and reader is established by the first-person form and reinforced by the final interrogative sentence of the body copy: 'I got the job, didn't I.' The only person in a position to answer is the reader.

Adverts which exploit the 'gossip' structure seem to fit very well into the actantial model for the analysis of the content of texts (cf. pp. 27-32). It needs to be only slight adapted in order to accommodate the female friend in this first subtype:

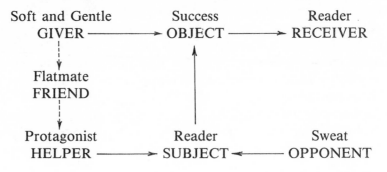

Soft and Gentle   Success   Reader
   GIVER ⎯⎯⎯⎯⎯→ OBJECT ⎯⎯⎯⎯→ RECEIVER

  Flatmate
  FRIEND

Protagonist   Reader   Sweat
HELPER ⎯⎯⎯⎯⎯→ SUBJECT ◄⎯⎯⎯ OPPONENT

Plate 20   Soft & Gentle,
She *August 1977.* © *Colgate-Palmolive Ltd. 1977*

We have not found even one advert with this structure addressing a male readership.

(b) *The core structure*   The presence of the protagonist's friend is an optional element in 'gossip' adverts; even without it they still retain their basic exploitation of the 'gossip' group. In adverts of this subtype the protagonist is still in charge of the total message, which is her personal testimony to the reader.

Within this category we find the Simplicity advert dealt with above (plate 12), where an ordinary woman addresses the female readers as her confidential friends. The personal testimony of the first-person narrator may become even more confidential when the picture shows a calendar page with a personal handwritten note or a diary entry. Such devices create an impression of letting you into the most secret wishes and experiences of the author. You become the direct confidante of the protagonist; there is no intermediary telling the story, and so, for example, you may be drawn into a group of women scheming to catch or outwit a handsome male. You can trust a diary because nothing in it is intended to be seen by others, it is written without any intention to deceive. Although the claim made for the product is improbable, the form of the advert is designed to make you suspend your disbelief — at least to the extent of catching at the straw of 'maybe'.

The protagonist may also be chosen for her authority with the general public as an expert or a celebrity. This is illustrated in a perfume advert which relies on the image of femininity represented by a famous actress: the perfume is 'soft, playful, wonderfully unpredictable. [It] is me — maybe it's you too.'

An advert for Yeast-Vite (*Titbits*, July 1977) relies on the expert knowledge of Angela Bradshaw, but in its total effect it balances between the expert image and that of one ordinary woman addressing another. To begin with, she addresses the reader as a friend-in-distress, creating a tone of intimacy through demonstrative pronouns which imply a shared experience between addresser and addressee: 'How can you stand that noise?' and 'There is something you can do the moment you feel that vague sense of oppression that heralds a headache.' At this moment, the expert takes over, which is signalled in the imperative verbs: 'Go straight to the medicine chest.' *She* knows the rational, no-fuss way to solve the problem, and you become the child-in-distress obeying your wiser mother.

This subtype is rarely found in men's magazines.

(c) *The derived structure*   Adverts in this category have no protagonist in charge of the total message, but include an *assistant
communicator* to support the message articulated by the advertiser.
When they occur in women's magazines — in which cases the assistant
communicator is usually a woman — these adverts may appeal to the
same 'gossip' tradition as the previous two categories, especially when
they attempt to strike a note of intimacy.

The advert for Vichy Skin Care (plate 21) falls into this category,
drawing on the testimony of Marianne Patten, an airline stewardess.
The image of intimacy and honesty is created partly through a
demonstrative pronoun: 'You see the advertisements with these
marvellous looking models'; and partly through her use of subdued
recommendations and understatements: her skin has 'really been more
stable' and Vichy has made 'a great deal of difference'. Incidentally,
this advert also mentions 'a friend' who told Marianne Patten about
Vichy.

In some cases, the advertiser simulates female intimacy through
verbal devices which give authority to a message communicated
without an assistant communicator. The following advert uses the
'inclusive we' in order to create an identity of interest for producer
and consumer: 'The way most of us treat our legs is pretty grim. To
remove unwanted hair, we still. . .' (*Cosmopolitan*, July 1977). The
advert then goes on to describe 'the ugly method' of hair removal:
'You know the routine' — a phrase whose imprecision presupposes
a shared knowledge between addresser and addressee. Adverts which
use an assistant communicator primarily as a source of factual
evidence of commodity advantages are not specific to women's
magazines.

(d) *The reversed structure*   In this category, which occurs very
rarely, adverts pretend that a reader has initiated a 'gossip' contact,
requesting reliable advice on an urgent personal problem. 'Dear Sally
Hansen Nail Experts, How can I give myself a professional manicure
at home. I've heard that it's not hard to have beautifully manicured
nails but I'm not sure' (plate 22). This reader's request is authenticated
by the form in which it appears: a personal, handwritten letter, partly
concealed by an array of Sally Hansen bottles. Altruistically, Sally
Hansen uses this opportunity to inform all the two million
Cosmopolitan readers of the seven steps which will make their mails
'look like a professional did them'.

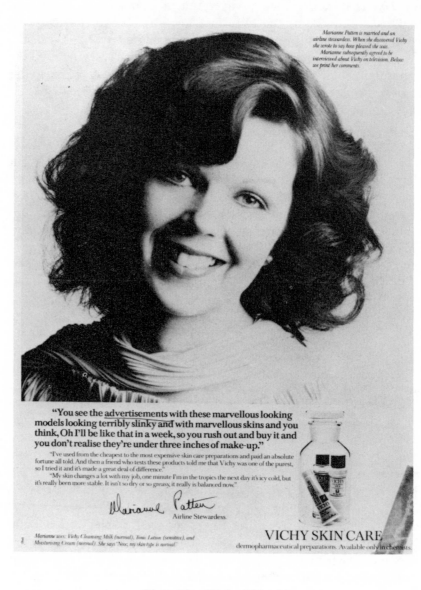

Plate 21   Vichy Skin Care
She April 1977

Dear Sally Hansen® Nail Experts, How can I give myself a professional manicure at home?

Just follow these steps and your nails will look like a professional did them.

Step one: remove nail colour	Sally Hansen fast-acting nail colour <u>Remover</u> gently conditions while it removes nail colour completely.
Step two: remove excess cuticles	Proteinized <u>Cuticle Remover</u> is the fast and safe way to remove excess cuticles.
Step three: moisturise and condition	Apply <u>Nail Treatment Cream</u> to restore essential moisture and help condition nails and cuticles.
Step four: apply base coat	Brush on <u>Nail Smoother</u>, the ridge-filling base coat that gives nails a smooth, even surface and helps nail colour wear longer.
Step five: colour and help strengthen	<u>Hard-As-Nails</u> patented nylon formula helps strengthen problem nails and helps keep them from splitting, chipping or cracking.
Step six: apply top coat	<u>Supershine</u> is a clear, top coat that protects nail colour and adds extra brilliance and shine.
Step seven: if you're in a hurry	Use <u>Dry Fast</u> to help prevent nail colour from smudging as it dries.

© 1981 Del Laboratories, Inc.

Sally Hansen®

Creators of Hard-As-Nails,® America's number one nail protection.
SALLY HANSEN LTD, 55 New Bond Street, London W1.
Available in the Republic of Ireland.

Plate 22   Sally Hansen
Cosmopolitan *October 1981*

The multiple identity?

A type of advert which we've only found in women's magazines uses the multiple lay-out page to represent different aspects of a person. Usually, half a dozen photos of the same woman engaged in various activities are spread over the page, each accompanied by an anchoring verbal text (cf. p. 34).

A good example is found in a Max Factor advert (plate 23) which shows us 24 hours in a woman's life in nine photos anchored in time: '9AM', '11.30AM', through to '2.50AM', '9AM'. The message is that the new Max Factor mascara 'lasts for 24 hours. . . Drive to work with the top down, play tennis or go for a swim.'

Judith Williamson, noting that 'the mulitple-identity type of ad is particularly relevant in relation to women' (1978: 57), tries to explain why this is so:

[The multiple-identity ad] provides a way for ads to incorporate potential criticisms, and flaws in their own system of meaning. This applies especially to their attitude to women, who have for so long been seen as one 'feminine' entity by advertisements. The idea of 'Women's Lib' has filtered into ads in that they are determined to show that their product suits not only all kinds of women but all the kinds of women within you.

(ibid.)

However, as Williamson observes, the assimilation of criticism has no or few liberating aspects, since the facet-pictures also simplify and limit the activities of women.

We therefore tend to favour another explanation which is inspired by Goffman's account (1979) of the similarity between childish behaviour and advertising images of women. Women in adverts often act in ways which are normally reserved for children, presenting themselves 'in puckish styling' (Goffman 1979: 48), with bashful facial or body positions, or generally careless behaviour approaching 'a sort of body clowning', using 'the entire body as a playful, gesticulative device' (Goffman 1979: 50). These descriptions seem to fit at least two of the photos of the Max Factor advert.

According to Goffman such features point to a general unseriousness of female behaviour, 'a readiness to be present in a social situation garbed and styled in a manner to which one isn't deeply or irrevocably committed [. . .] as though life were a series of costume

MAX FACTOR INVENTS
THE 24-HOUR MASCARA

9AM

11.30AM

2.45PM

4.15PM

6.35PM

8.50PM

12.35AM

2.50AM

9AM

New! Maxi-Lash
24-HOUR MASCARA

A mascara that lasts for 24 hours? You can even sleep in it and wake up with great looking lashes. No, we're not kidding.

Drive to work with the top down, play tennis or go for a swim. Maxi-Lash 24-hour mascara is waterproof. Smudgeproof. Smearproof. Flakeproof.

New! Maxi-Frost
LONG-LASTING SHADOW

And if you're wild about shine, wear new long lasting Maxi-Frost shadow. It's rich in gleamy colour, stays put for hours.

Cosmo, 1977

Only by **MAX FACTOR**

Plate 23   Max Factor
Cosmopolitan *April 1977*

balls. Thus, occasionally one can mock one's own appearance, for identification is not deep' (Goffman 1979: 51). One should not forget, however, that the young woman's lack of commitment to the various roles (in adverts) is only possible against a background of traditional female roles, which (it is implied) any woman must be serious about sooner or later in life. The additional roles may be fun, but they don't require genuine involvement.

This explanation of the multiple lay-out adverts has the advantage of excluding those rare male-addressed (usually car) adverts which describe different aspects of a man's life in two or three photos. In no such case do we find a lack of role-commitment. 'Each guise seems to afford him something he is totally serious about, and deeply identified with, as though wearing a skin, not a costume' (ibid.).

ADDRESSING MEN

The ideal of femininity

Women rarely appear in adverts addressed to a male audience; when they do, the portrayal of the female sex testifies to the fact that the female characteristics most appreciated by men are an acknowledgement of inferiority and dependence, and a readiness to serve men.

Male-addressed adverts tend to portray women in two basic ways: as a whore and as a servant, although there is a tendency for male daydreams to conflate the two.

The role as whore is most explicit in massage adverts. One promises a return to the days of Roman splendour and offers a host of beautiful girls who will pamper tired bodies in the way that Romans demanded. Another advert promises that 'after your flight (or busy business day)' you can relax with masseuses who are 'attractive looking, intelligent and well-spoken, well-dressed and 23-33 years old...all races, all colours — but all cultured, all very very good' (*Mayfair*, August 1977).

Also adverts for more ordinary 'commodities' appeal to the male fondness for sexually compliant girls, although the association between commodity and sexy women has to be inferred by the reader from visual and/or verbal allusions. An example is provided by an advert for tobacco which pictures a handsome, tough male in a dressing gown exposing his chest, with a relayed text claiming that this tobacco is the only fragrance a man needs. The reader asking himself 'for what?' need only glance at the scantily clad woman waiting in the background in order to complete the elliptic caption.

The servant aspect is dominant in an advert for Singapore Airlines (*Newsweek*, December 1981) — although the sexual aspect is by no means absent. The sweet Asian air-hostess is pictured reclining in exotic surroundings as she is replying to a letter-poem which she has received from an infatuated passenger praising the

> Gentle hostess in your sarong kebaya
> you care for me as only you know how
> . . .
> Singapore girl
> you're a great way to fly.

In a more recent Singapore Airlines advert (*Time*, September 1982) the persuasive element is much more latent: the role of the sweet air-hostess has been reduced to a smiling face in the bottom right corner, while two naked women have been retouched as silhouettes into the ice-cubes of the very prominent cocktail. The efficiency of such 'subliminal seduction' (cf. Key, 1973) is a much disputed issue: most people do not, and are not meant to, become aware of the ecstatic women in the ice-cubes. But does our lewd subconscious nevertheless register these images, disposing us favourably towards Singapore Airlines? Maybe this is the justification for boasting an 'inflight service even other airlines talk about'?

Advertising like this has often drawn criticism from women. Sarah Mower (1981) sees such adverts as evidence that 'despite our progress over the last decade, the portrayal of women in advertisements is often sexist and demeaning', especially in trade and industrial journals, car and motorbike magazines, and 'girlie' magazines.

Offensive adverts also occur quite frequently in women's magazines, however; an advert for shoes is sexually aggressive, like many shoe adverts. It displays the upper part of two women's thighs, baring seven inches of skin between the extremely brief pants and the sophisticated knitted stockings which reach just above the knee. Many women would probably find it degrading to see their sex portrayed as a detached pelvis with legs, especially since this portrayal is not justified in relation to the shoes advertised.[2]

Mower's article expresses the wish that it should be made possible to 'weed out' offensive and degrading adverts in magazines. We are not in favour of this proposal, not because we are opposed to attempts at regulating advertising, but because a regulation must have a more general scope in order to be operational (cf. pp. 168 ff.). How exactly would one decide which adverts are and are not degrading or offensive to women? And if a group of women like Women in Media were to have jurisdiction over adverts portraying women, then what about adverts protraying men as sexual animals (cf. below)? Since such male images can only be realized at the expense of women, such adverts may also be called 'offensive to women'?

The ideal of masculinity

The predominance of subservient women can be seen to reflect a male longing for those unproblematic days when their sovereignty was uncontested and no adamant feminists demanded changes in men's behaviour and attitudes. Not surprisingly, this image of woman is complemented by an image of masculinity designed to bolster the male ego.

Frequently man is pictured as a sexual animal, right from the almost embarrassed allusions of a Martini advert — which assures us that we can drink Martini 'before and after sailing, golf, riding. Before and after . . . just about anything' (*Mayfair*, October 1977) — to more explicit invitations to 'make every day your Brut day', 'Carry a big stick' and 'Give it your best shot' (adverts for Brut aftershave, stick deodorant and anti-perspirant spray, respectively) (*Playboy's Fashion Guide*, spring/summer 1981).

This brutish image is taken to its logical conclusion in an English Leather Musk advert whose headline tells us that Musk by English Leather is 'the civilized way to roar', illustrated by a figure half man, half lion, whose stare is unmistakably 'Earthy. Primitive. Fiercely masculine' (plate 24).

Another advert adopts the same means of persuasion, reminding the male that it's a jungle out there. Tarzan should follow his instincts and aim for a wild, untamed virile look. The picture shows a fashionable Tarzan of the 1980s, prowling with his tiger by night.

The animal image is sometimes inflected towards the strong, vigorous, tough man, as in an advert for a Greek alcoholic drink which claims that it is something that not every man can handle. Besides

Plate 24   *English Leather Musk*
Viva

invoking the competitive aspect of male relationships, it plays upon the possession of relentless physical strength: the picture shows an armoured knight's iron glove clasping a bottle and this image is played upon in the copy.

This last advert bridges the gap between two images of masculinity: man competitive for women, and man competitive for success in the traditionally male fields of operation — business and politics, with the objectives of money and power. The success image can be illustrated by an advert for cigars, picturing a well-groomed man stylishly dressed in an expensive hunting outfit: 'When you've got the taste for leadership, light up an A & C Grenadier' (*Penthouse*, September 1980). In the well-known series of Rothmans adverts, now no longer used, a whole type of man is metonymically represented by a hairy, tanned hand (e.g. plate 25). This hand of a pilot, together with the slogan 'When you know what you want', appeals both to the reader's discrimination with respect to cigarettes and to the more general aims in life which are visually condensed in the picture — wealth, power, control.

There are a few traces in adverts of a more relaxed attitude to the necessity for men to be superior to women in traditionally male spheres like mechanics and technology. An advert for Scottish Widows life insurance, which appeared in the *Sunday Times Magazine* (half of whose readers are men), breaks both advertising and sex-role conventions in order to attract attention to a dull message. The headline '0 to 5 m.p.h. in 20 secs.' makes fun of the more virile car adverts, while the photo of a man pushing an old Ford Anglia and the beginning of the body copy picture a situation which is embarrasing for the male ego:

There you are trying to impress her with your racing starts and double declutches when the car stalls and you have to get out and push. 'that's second gear,' you tell her. Then when you've caught up with her she tells you the mixture's too rich, the firing's uneven and you should really sell it while it's still going.

(*Sunday Times Magazine*, July 1977)

Nevertheless, presupposing that the advert succeeds in catching attention without antagonizing the reader, the message of female technological superiority works as an attention-catcher only because it deviates from the sex role norms.

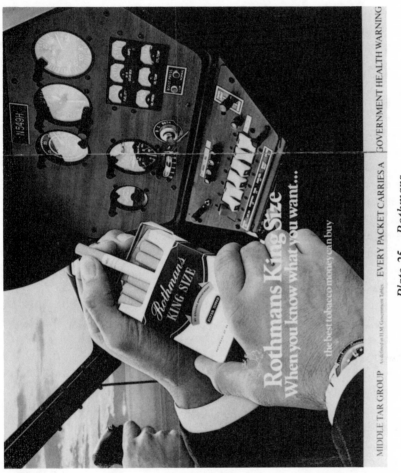

Plate 25 Rothmans
Mayfair *August 1977*

ADDRESSING MEN AND WOMEN: CONCLUSION

Advertising invites men and women to engage in an almost theatrically self-directed sex role behaviour, most explicitly sexual for men, who are accorded an uncontrollable sexual instinct in our culture; more indirectly sexual for women, who have only in the last century or so won the right to possess a sexuality.

Especially in adverts addressed to women, we seldom find unequivocal traces of a passionate sexuality; a rare example is in one for lipstick (*Cosmopolitan*, July 1977) boasting 'a luscious seductive sheen' and 'Sun kissed colours that look lastingly tempting'.

In the archetypal division of women into madonna (pure, gentle, artless, white) and whore (passionate, temptress, red), the advertising ideal of a 'natural' woman comes closer to a modestly liberated version of the madonna: still gentle and passive, but sexually attractive (though not aggressive), like the woman in the Lancôme advert (plate 26) — a fresh young flower (the floral dress and hat, the foliage) anxiously waiting for the man she loves, but bashful enough to cast down her countenance when she's with him.

This is the definition of a 'natural' woman, quite irrespective of the number of times she has violated the madonna feature of artlessness by using artificial beauty products in order to become attractive. For men, sexual potency is depicted as the epitome of masculinity.

Even in *Cosmopolitan* adverts the liberated woman subordinates herself to the man. This is aptly illustrated by the perfume advert discussed above (p. 96), picturing an active, intellectual, beautiful and independent woman. However, in the top left inset photo where she and a man are riding the same horse, he is holding the reins. Whenever the sexes are together, the man remains in control. Moreover, this inset photo is the only one in the advert which doesn't use soft focus; hence the subordinate woman is visually 'in focus'.

Advertising, then, seems to interpret the movement towards female equality largely as a moderate sexual liberation whose function is to legitimize pre- and possibly extra-marital affairs.

Lancôme create

Ô

The anytime,
anywhere
fragrance

Ô de Lancôme.
The anytime, anywhere fragrance.
It's light.
Refreshing.
Bringing your whole body alive
with sparkling vitality. Reviving
that early morning freshness.
The whole day through.
Ô de Lancôme.
The anytime, anywhere fragrance.
Also available as a double
concentration spray.

THE FRENCH HAVE A WORD FOR BEAUTY

LANCÔME

Plate 26   Lancôme
Cosmopolitan *July 1977*

ADDRESSING THE CLASSES

Publicity principally addressed to the working class tends to promise a personal transformation through the function of the particular product it is selling (Cinderella); middle-class publicity promises a transformation of relationships through a general atmosphere created by an ensemble of products (The Enchanted Palace).

(Berger 1972: 145)

This quotation from *Ways of Seeing* certainly suggests an interesting hypothesis of class-specific advertising. However, Berger does not support the hypothesis with a detailed analysis, and it becomes extremely difficult for others to check the hypothesis when he doesn't specify the defining features of working-class and middle-class adverts — apart from giving one example of each. Nevertheless, advertisers — and critical scholars — have to take into account the class membership and class identifications of the audience of the various publications.

In Marxist terms we may distinguish between two primary classes: the bourgeoisie, which privately owns and controls the means of production, but which is too small to play any part in advertising strategies; opposed to the bourgeoisie is the working class with its many internal divisions forming the overwhelming majority.

All readership surveys, however, are based on a class model which includes six classes: lower-, middle- and upper-working class and lower-, middle- and upper-middle class (which all belong to the working class in the definition just given). This model reflects the way in which people normally think of classes as a sliding scale of social stratification rather than as an antagonistic division between bourgeoisie and working class.

In our discussion of class-specific advertising we shall have to use this stratification model, distinguishing between a working class consisting of manual, skilled or unskilled blue-collar workers, and a middle class consisting of non-manual white-collar workers, including those with secretarial jobs, the professional classes and civil servants.

Irrespective of a given individual's membership of a specific social stratum, he or she has a relative freedom to respond to his or her social position and situation in terms of at least three meaning systems:[3]

1 *The dominant system.* This presents what might be called the 'official' version of class relations. It promotes endorsement of the existing inequality, and leads to a response among members of the subordinate class that can be described either as *deferential*, or as *aspirational*. That is, a 'dominant' definition of the situation leads people to accept the existing distribution of jobs, power, wealth, etc. Either they simply defer to 'the way things are', or they aspire to an individual share of the available rewards.

2 *The subordinate system.* This defines a moral framework which, while prepared to endorse the dominant system's claims to overall control of the economic processes, nevertheless reserves the right to negotiate a better share for particular groups at any time. It promotes *accommodative* or *negotiated* responses to inequality, and can be seen at work for instance in the attitudes behind the notion of 'them' and 'us', and in the collective bargaining of trade-unionism, whereby the *framework* of the reward structure is accepted. All that is at issue is the share to be had by various communities or groups.

3 *The radical system.* The source for this is the mass political party based on that section of the subordinate class whose identity of interest is expressed in working-class solidarity. It is class-conscious (unlike the previous two meaning systems) in that it rejects the frameworks by which one class achieves a dominant position, and so it promotes an *oppositional* response to inequality.

(Fiske and Hartley 1978: 104)

As stated above, individuals have a relative freedom to respond to their social situation in terms of these meaning systems, they may even move between the systems: 'Each one of us holds mutually contradictory beliefs about our position in society, and we respond to our condition in different ways at the same time' (Fiske and Hartley 1978: 103).

However, for the present purposes we may venture to generalize and say that there exists a rough correspondence between, on the one hand, a traditional middle-class consciousness and the dominant system. The members of this class are relatively privileged in terms of wealth, power and opportunities, which may lead to an acceptance of the competitive individualist ideology. Since they have achieved some sort of status, away from the bottom of the social hierarchy, this ideology has a certain credibility for them.

On the other hand, we see a rough correspondence between a traditional working-class consciousness and the subordinate system.

Many members of the working class dispassionately accept their position at the bottom of the class structure, because the experience of generations has taught them that 'working-class kids get working-class jobs'. Some resign themselves to a defeatist attitude, others put their energies into a reformist struggle for the collective improvement of their class conditions.

If these correspondences are justified, we should expect adverts addressing a middle-class audience to stress the aspirational response (cf. p. 61). This is indeed the case in numerous middle-class adverts, which appeal to the individuality of their readers, singling out each audience member as a unique individual, sometimes to the extent of picturing women as solipsists, staring into the void or narcissistically enjoying their own bodies. The individualism is most explicit in the verbal parts of the ads:

> [Brand X cereal] breakfast is specially for people who want to improve their shape but not completely redesign it.
>
> > (*She*, August 1977)

> Cancan [...] for the woman who dares to live life to the full.
>
> > (ibid.)

> After all, you could say we had you in mind when we made it.
>
> > (ibid.)

> Then again, [Volvo] was never meant to be a car for any but the discriminating few.
>
> > (*Time*, September 1982)

Sometimes, middle-class adverts flatter their audience by implying that they already belong to a prestigious social group, for instance the regular winter holiday makers:

> Choosing your skiing holiday this year [...] could be easier than it's ever been before.
>
> > (*Sunday Times Magazine*, July 1977)

Nevertheless, flattery of the reader's ego is not entirely absent from working-class adverts:

Whatever kind of hair you have, one is just right for you.
(*Woman*, July 1977)

Imperial International...for those who demand perfection.
(*Mayfair*, October 1977)

When we analyse adverts addressing a working-class audience, we find practically no trace of the accommodative response which belongs to 'the subordinate system' (cf. above), not to mention the oppositional response, which is totally absent, for obvious reasons: advertising cannot seriously use a response which rejects the entire socioeconomic structure on which advertising depends. Therefore, when once in a while they refer to oppositional responses, adverts are designed to neutralize such responses (cf. pp. 163 ff.).

Even the accommodative response seems to be largely incompatible with the aims of advertising: in seeking to persuade each individual reader of the personal benefits to be achieved through the purchase of the commodity, or of the miraculous capacity of a commodity to compensate for what is perceived as a personal shortcoming, advertising has no room for the vague associations of group solidarity of the subordinate system.

A Pyrex advert (plate 27) does indeed exploit the notion of 'them' and 'us' in the use of 'what' as a relative pronoun referring to human beings, which is a distinctive feature of working-class speech; it also refers to 'upstairs people'. But its whole aim is to get working-class readers to identify with the upstairs people whose liking for Pyrex casseroles allegedly caused them to give up their servants (see also p. 163). In spite of its inclusion of the accommodative response, therefore, the 'preferred meaning' of this advert leads the audience towards the dominant meaning system.

The vast majority of working-class adverts quite obviously assume that their readers have no other desire than to join the ranks of the middle class; advertising here acquires the function of a catalogue which enables aspiring working-class readers to keep in touch with the middle-class standards they want to copy. We can therefore see working-class advertising as founded on a wholesale adoption of the *embourgeoisement* thesis, 'which on the evidence of apparently widespread affluence in the 1960s sought to show that old class divisions were breaking down as members of the working class "joined" the middle class in increasing numbers' (Fiske and Hartley 1978: 106).

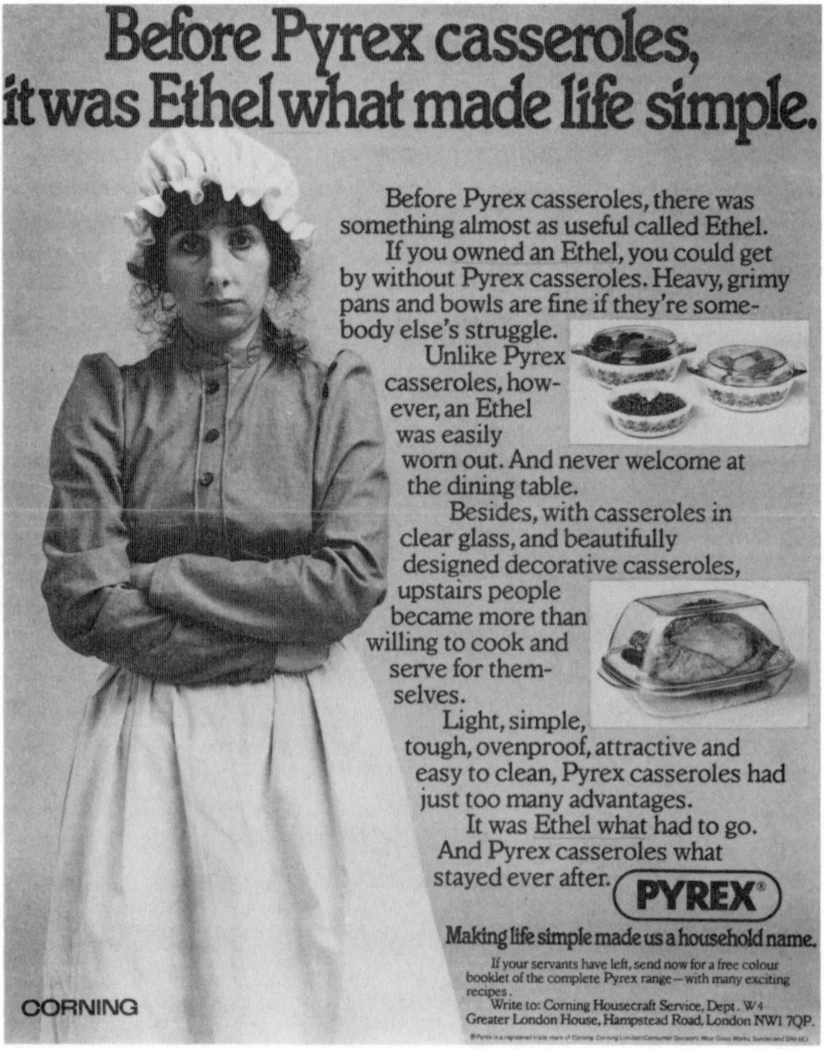

Plate 27   Pyrex
Woman October 1977

In other words, most adverts take for granted that your relative position in the status hierarchy is determined by the number of prestige products which you possess. For instance, an advert for Easifit stretch covers promises that 'Easifit adds that touch of class' (*Woman*, October 1977).

Taken in this sense, Berger's hypothesis that adverts addressing a working-class audience draw on the Cinderella myth is correct: many do offer a late-capitalist version of the personal transformation depicted by the tale of Cinderella. However, many middle-class adverts also offer their readers prestige through consumption.

On the other hand, if you do *not* possess a certain prestige object, your friends and neighbours will form a less respectful view of you. Some adverts deliberately play on this fear of the working-class upstarts that they will be unmasked, by offering the attributes for creating a pretentious veneer on their original non-prestigious identity.

An advert for Nairn Cushionflor illustrates this strategy, the body copy beginning:

> You'd be amazed how much your friends can see of you
> every time they walk into your bathroom. All they've
> got to do is take a look on the floor. The flooring you
> choose to put down says a lot about the sort of person
> you are.
>
> (*Woman*, October 1977)

Besides giving the *Mayfair* reader punning references to a touch of class, an advert for a brand of cigars confidentially advises that a little name-dropping can be very effective, and offers the brand-name for this treatment.

This advice is designed to appeal to the social insecurity of any working-class upstart, since 'name-dropping' is typically necessary for the person who doesn't feel accepted as an equal and who wants to create an impression of something which is not really him.

Finally, an advert for a car radio illustrates a third variation on the same theme.

> Everyone is switching from radio to full in-car stereo;
> but with so many to choose from, the problem is which
> one?
>
> (*Titbits*, July 1977)

While being particularly typical of working-class adverts, this example exploits a general characteristic of consumer society: the importance of doing what everybody else is doing, in short, the importance of keeping up with the Joneses.

5

Advertising as a
Psychological Mirror

INTRODUCTION

Most people would probably agree that many individual consumer adverts function on the level of the day-dream. By picturing quite unusually happy and glamorous people whose success in either career or sexual terms, or both, is obvious, adverts construct an imaginary world in which the reader is able to make come true those desires which remain unsatisfied in his or her everyday life.

An advert for a science fiction magazine is unusually explicit about this. In addition to the primary use value of the magazine, the reader is promised access to a wonderful universe through the product — access to other mysterious and tantalizing worlds and epochs, the realms of the imagination. When studying advertising, it is therefore unreasonable to expect readers to decipher adverts as factual statements about reality. Most adverts are just too meagre in informative content and too rich in emotional suggestive detail to be read literally. If people read then literally, they would soon be forced to realize their error when the glamorous promises held out by the adverts didn't materialize.

It is in connection with this problem of the credibility of advertising (or 'publicity' as he calls it) that Berger comes up with the day-dream as the concept which enables us to understand the readers' response to advertising:

Glamour cannot exist without personal social envy being a common and widespread emotion. The industrial society which has moved towards democracy and then stopped half way is the ideal society for generating such an emotion. The pursuit of individual happiness has been acknowledged as a universal right. Yet the existing social conditions make the individual feel powerless. He lives in the contradiction between what he is and what he would like to be. Either he then becomes fully conscious of the contradiction and its causes, and so joins the political struggle for a full democracy which entails, amongst other things, the overthrow of capitalism; or else he lives continually subject to an envy which, compounded with his sense of powerlessness, dissolves into recurrent day-dreams.

It is this which makes it possible to understand why publicity remains credible. The gap between what publicity actually offers and the future it promises, corresponds with the gap between what the spectator-buyer feels himself to be and what he would like to be. The two gaps become one; and instead of the single gap being bridged by action or lived experience, it is filled with glamorous day-dreams.

(Berger 1972: 148)

The average consumer is not surprised that his purchase of the commodity does not redeem the promise of the advertisement, for this is what he is used to in life: the individual's pursuit of happiness and success is usually in vain. But the fantasy is his to keep; in his dream-world he enjoys a 'future endlessly deferred' (Berger 1972: 146).

The Estivalia advert (plate 28) is quite explicit about the fact that advertising shows us not reality, but a fantasy; it does so by openly admitting the day-dream but in a way which insists on the existence of a bridge linking day-dream to reality — Estivalia, which is 'for daydream believers', those who refuse to give up trying to make the hazy ideal of natural beauty and harmony come true.

If adverts function on the day-dream level, it clearly becomes inadequate to merely condemn advertising for channelling readers' attention and desires towards an unrealistic, paradisial nowhere land. Advertising certainly does that, but in order for people to find it relevant, the utopia visualized in adverts must be linked to our surrounding reality by a causal connection.

By compensating for the dreariness of everyday life through fantasies, advertising inevitably becomes evidence of the dreariness of everyday life. In picturing people as they may become, adverts cannot help showing by implication, in a kind of reversed mirror, what people are not at present. Or, to push the argument a little, if advertising pictures people as beautiful, happy, socially secure

estivalia – an enchanting new fragrance. Now available in the UK from selected perfumery outlets. Eau de toilette, eau de toilette spray and atomiser, deodorant spray, lait de beauté, soap.

Plate 28   Estivalia
Cosmopolitan *July 1977*

and successful, does it not follow that people subconsciously experience themselves as ugly, miserable, isolated and frustrated?

By inviting us to enter its imaginary paradise, advertising thus becomes a magic mirror in which a more subtle interpretation enables us to discern the contours of widespread popular discontent with everyday life and with the opportunities provided by the society in which we live. Advertising is therefore founded on a subconscious desire for a better world.

Below (cf. pp. 133-8 and chapter 6) we shall return to the ways in which advertising diverts the readers' attention away from the need for radical changes in the socioeconomic structure and instead provides us with blinkers which make us focus on the capital interest of advertising: individualist consumption.

TAKING THE IDEOLOGICAL TEMPERATURE

Before we go on to develop the Utopian elements of advertising any further, it is necessary to say a few words about the purpose of analysing adverts in this way. All mass media are dependent on the co-operation of their readers for their success; right from the act of buying a magazine people play an active role in mass communication, bringing their socially created individual needs to the medium concerned. The 'reading' process itself requires both energy and interpretative skills — think for instance of puns which can be quite hard to work out. Why should people bother if they got nothing out of it, if somehow the meaning communicated didn't correspond to the attitudes, hopes and dreams of those reading media messages?

The content of the mass media can therefore be seen as a celebration of common experiences, of socially shared dreams and hopes, which are validated for their readers by this celebration. Media messages are not just a matter of the consciousness industry addressing millions of isolated individuals; instead, like the TV messages described by Fiske and Hartley, media messages in general are decoded.

according to individually learnt but culturally generated codes and conventions, which of course impose similar constraints of perception on the encoders of the messages. It seems, then, that television [and other mass media — our insertion] functions as a social ritual, overriding individual distinctions in which our culture engages, in order to communicate with its collective self.

(Fiske and Hartley 1978: 85).

For unashamedly commercial media like advertising, it is absolutely essential to be in contact with the readers' consciousness, first in order to catch their attention, and secondly to dispose them favourably towards the product advertised. Advertisers therefore have to please the readers, never disturb or offend them; and because adverts are under this obligation to reflect the attitudes, hopes and dreams of their readers as closely as possible, we can gain an insight into the readers' consciousness, their ways of thinking, their ideology, by analysing the structures of meaning found in advertisements. Through an analysis of advertising it becomes possible to take the temperature of popular ideology; for instance an advert for two types of canned chinese food testifies to the widespread racism in Britain. Assuring prospective buyers that 'Here are two orientals you'll want to invite to dinner again and again' (*Woman*, August 1977), the advert carries the expectation (cf. pp. 24 ff.) that normally orientals are *not* welcome at your table and, by treating this prejudiced attitude as the most natural thing, helps to legitimate it.

On the other hand, advertising also has to incorporate currents of social discontent which may threaten industry's freedom of action and ultimately even the basic principles of the economic system. When the worries of ordinary people about, say, pollution reach a certain level of urgency, advertising has to incorporate such popular concern, both in order to demonstrate its sensitivity to consumer anxieties and in order to appease popular opinions by vaguely conceding that something must be done about it. Such lip-service sensitivity is illustrated in a menstrual protection advert assuring the readers that 'both the tampon and its container-applicator are flushable and biodegradable. This makes good sense ecologically' (*Cosmopolitan*, July 1977).

This notion of taking the current ideological temperature may appear to be an unnecessarily indirect way of acquiring knowledge of prevalent social attitudes — why not simply ask people what they believe, what their ideals and hopes are? The answer is that people do not always have access to their most deep-rooted attitudes and beliefs — in fact a person's ideology can be defined as those values which he takes for granted in a communication situation, those values which are so self-evident that they needn't be articulated at all (cf. chapter 6). Therefore, the most coherent, accessible version of the popular ideological universe can be found in the textual messages which people consume regularly, because they find pleasure in them.

The expression 'ideological temperature' should be regarded as an abstraction — indeed the parallel to human physiology implies that ideology, like body temperature, is never static but continuously changing, in a complex cultural process. However, this account, like any description of an ideological complex, has to assume that ideology can be fixed in a momentary standstill.

Such a standstill is in fact potentially present in advertising messages; always wanting to be able to control the future in order to plan the smooth production and sale of commodities, advertising is constantly trying to preserve time-honoured, stabilizing formulas and values and the current status quo against new practices and attitudes. When new sentiments achieve a breakthrough, in spite of advertising and other conservative factors, the industry is quick to adjust; for instance there has been a demonstrable change in advertising's portrayal of sex roles, a change towards greater equality which the advertising industry certainly didn't initiate and which it is doing its best to deflect and arrest (cf. the advert for Cabriole, plate 39).

THE UTOPIA OF YOUTH AND LEISURE

At the beginning of this chapter we made it clear that advertising doesn't simply reflect the real world as we experience it: the world portrayed in advertisements moves on a day-dream level, which implies a dissatisfaction with the real world expressed through imaginary representations of the future as it might be: a Utopia.

The overrepresentation in adverts, established in many studies, of youth vs. age, leisure vs. work, beauty vs. ugliness, and so on, must be interpreted not as straightforward statements about the everyday world, but as a symbolic representation of the social esteem accorded to the young, the free and the beautiful, and as people's wishful thinking about their own future.

Interpreted in this way, adverts reflect widespread social values and attitudes with respect to the means and ends of human activities. This is succinctly expressed by Fiske and Hartley in their description of the symbolic messages of TV-series: 'The world of television is clearly different from our real social world, but just as clearly related to it in some way. We might clarify this relationship by saying that television does not represent the manifest actuality of our society, but rather reflects, symbolically, the structure of values and relationships beneath the surface' (Fiske and Hartley 1978: 24).

Thus the overrepresentation of young people should be seen not as a distortion of a social fact, but as an indicator that old age is held in low esteem in our culture. Our work-ethic-based and rapidly developing society attaches so much importance to efficiency and flexibility that in many jobs people over 40—45 are just no good any more; the experience which they have acquired through their working lives has long since become obsolete. However, the apparent need, deduced from the advertising, for youth and strength may on a deeper level be interpreted as a longing for a society which holds old age in higher esteem.

In the same manner, the high proportion of leisure situations should be seen as evidence not of a dislike of work as such, but as antipathy towards work as exploited, regimented and mono-tonized by contemporary industrial capitalism; against the absurd situation where not having a job is experienced as meaningless, while those fortunate enough to have a job rarely expect or demand meaningfulness from their work. The apparent need for leisure and escape from work may therefore be interpreted as a subconscious need for meaningful, self-managed work.

However, these potentially subversive elements remain latent in the advertising universe because they are always embedded within structures of meaning which stay loyal to the present socioeconomic system. Seen in this context the promise of a holiday advert that 'you're *free* to *enjoy* yourself' (*Sunday Times Magazine*, July 1977) becomes a symptom of a working life whose coercion and drudgery you can do nothing to change, only escape from through the (bi-)annual holiday. While incorporating vaguely subversive ten-dencies, advertising thus functions basically as a bulwark against social change by disseminating what are presented as 'the rules of the game' — those norms and types of behaviour which are presented as self-evident and inviolable for all who want to lead a normal human life. Many adverts depend for their fascination on promising a temporary transcendence of the norms (see the MG advert, plate 33), which makes it even more important to become aware of these norms which are so fundamental as to allow only a temporary release. It is these seemingly natural and inevitable rules of life which we term 'ideological'. Before dealing with them in greater depth (cf. chapter 6), we shall have a closer look at individual adverts in which the frustrations of contemporary life surface as problems to be solved by the products or services offered by the advertisers.

ADVERTISEMENTS AS A
SOCIO-PSYCHOLOGICAL DIAGNOSIS

Loneliness

The first advertisement to be dealt with in this section is a symptom of the deprivations of urban life (see plate 29 from *She*, August 1977; an almost identical advert is found in *Mayfair*, October 1977). It presents its emergency solution to the widespread loneliness among young people as a desirable paradise of fun and fulfilment.

Addressing 'single and unattached' people who have mixed feelings about being both 'independent and free' and 'sometimes a little lonely and "cut-off"', the Singles Society promises to 'help you get the best out of single living'. Although the services offered by the Singles Society may be invaluable for desperately lonely people, the very existence of such services can be taken as evidence of and an implicit criticism of a society which is unable to provide meaningful patterns of interaction between people, and which has failed to produce social units which, so to speak, automatically cater for people's need for companionship and diversion in a genuine and intimate manner. In the words of another advert (*Cosmopolitan*, July 1977), 'In this age of modern technology and mass communication people are actually feeling lonely. But meeting new friends can be very difficult as people travel and move house more often.'

It's much more fun being single in company!

Plate 29   Singles Society
She *October 1977*

In former times people were integrated members of a social organism living their whole lives supported by the social network of a small community, characterized by the mutual help of and contact with family, friends, neighbours, local shopkeepers, and so on. They may have joined various clubs and associations organized around certain primary activities like sports or collective bargaining and, as a spill-over, secondary social activities arose. They didn't feel a need to belong, because they already belonged. In some cases individuals may have experienced the social network as exasperatingly restrictive, but they were never allowed to feel lonely; and occupying a fixed position in a static social hierarchy provided security, even when that position was a low one.[1]

The social and geographical mobility of contemporary society gives no security, partly because material affluence and increased leisure are not accompanied by more responsibility and control, partly because the majority are bound to fail when trying to be the architects of their own future.

When the geographical mobility of people migrating in large numbers in order to get a job or an education is added to a more dynamic social hierarchy, the result is anonymous urban people with no stable identity, deprived of close and lasting personal relations with other people, more and more dependent on the help of professional experts who try to attend to the functions previously taken care of by the social networks which have now disintegrated. This feeling of being a lonely island in the social ocean is skilfully exploited by an Automobile Association membership campaign which, in addition to the objective advantage for members of the free breakdown service, offers to satisfy the more intangible social needs of prospective members, because 'It's great to feel you belong' (*She*, August 1977).

The Singles Society advert can be seen as part of a general tendency in our society for 'specialist' commercial enterprises to take over all sorts of cultural activities which were previously dependent on people's initiative and imagination. Just as you may buy yourself a pre-cooked, frozen meal most of the ingredients of which are unknown to you, instead of mixing and cooking ingredients which you've brought home (or grown) yourself; so you may join a whole countrywide organization complete with 'regional organizers', 'Breakaway Weekends', 'discos', and so on, instead of arranging your own cheese and wine parties or picnics with people you know well and like.

What we are witnessing through this advert is a more and more alienated urban society where large commercial organizations are profiting directly from single people's need for company, by attaching them to one specific chain of holiday resorts, bars and other places of entertainment; a society where it has become necessary to formally arrange informal social gatherings for people with no other wish than somebody to talk to — although the advert's illustration picturing five overjoyed couples seems to suggest that people may also have the possibility of a more permanent relationship in mind. And since the Dateline marriage bureau is affiliated with the Singles Society, it doesn't appear too unlikely that by joining you may 'find that special someone you've always wanted to meet'.

The Singles Society, in its promise of a here-and-now solution, reduces the seriousness of the social network problem: it's really no problem at all if only you fill in the coupon and join 'like-minded single men and women'. The artificial social network is an extraneous organization of people's social lives which doesn't solve the basic problem of providing frames of life which make it possible for people themselves to play a part in the shaping of their work and out-of-work activities. Instead, joining the Singles Society is presented as the obvious, natural thing to do. As Williamson (1978: 14) observes, 'the need for relationship and human meaning appropriated by advertising is one that, if only it was not diverted, could radically change the society we live in'.

Insecurity

Another example of the breakdown of the social network is provided by an Abbey National building society advert (plate 30). Here the readers' attention is not focused on the loneliness of single people, but on the insecurity of the young family.

The advert addresses itself to the new parents' sense of responsibility and need for security: 'Security. And a new person totally dependent on you. The Abbey Habit can help you to the security you all need.' It relies for its effect on a puzzle of words to be deciphered by the reader, who really has to make an effort to make sense of the words partly hidden behind the baby's helpless, appealing eyes.

Security. It's worth more than you can measure.

Security. And a new person totally dependent on you. The Abbey Habit can help you to the security you all need. So come on in.

Get the Abbey Habit

WITH
ABBEY NATIONAL
and get some real security behind you

Most of our branches are open 9-5 daily PLUS Saturday mornings. Abbey National Building Society, Abbey House, Baker Street, London NW1 6XL.

Plate 30   Abbey National
Woman *October 1977*

It is not possible to reconstruct the whole text, which is quite peculiar: the words seemingly cut off by the page division or the baby's head must have been placed after the baby's head was filled in, since the illegible words are repeated in the following line(s) in order to achieve at least a minimum of comprehension. The keywords and phrases can be simultaneously applied to the relationship between parents and child and the relationship which Abbey National want to establish between themselves and the parents:

SECURITY. ALWAYS THERE IF NEEDED. SOMETHING BEHIND YOU. TOWER OF STRENGTH. MAINSTAY. SAFE.

Abbey National is thus trying to tie the reader to the building society by exploiting all the sincerity, tenderness and dependence invoked by the presence of the baby.

Clearly, the advert only makes sense if the services it offers can compensate for values which the reader's life is lacking: security, support, care, and so on, i.e. values which were almost automatically and mutually provided by the close-knit communities in former times. Therefore the advert will mainly affect people who feel left to their own devices, at the mercy of social forces which they neither understand nor control.

Tension

In the Pears foam bath advert (plate 31) a generally hectic lifestyle is a basic premise. Through Pears you can escape temporarily: you can make 'time all your own', 'let yourself be soothed', let 'the tensions slip away', make 'the world seem a nicer place'. All of this carries the expectation that the world is *not* a nice place, that the clock has become your master, that you are worried and tense. Nevertheless, you are asked to accept these phenomena; or rather, the possibility that they might be changed just doesn't get into the picture. But the strains of modern life become easier to endure when Pears is there to relieve you from time to time — especially since Pears takes into account that your mood may vary, by putting no less than three foam bath variants at your disposal: when you 'choose your fragrance to match your mood', your potential range of moods may comprise Country Herbs, Original Amber and Lemon Blossom!

PEARS FOAM BATH. THERE ISN'T A GENTLER PLACE YOU COULD BE.

Take a little time. And make it all your own. In a gentle, relaxing Pears Foam Bath.

Immerse your body in its gentle bubbling cleansers made from natural oils.
Let yourself be soothed by its fresh, clean fragrance.

As the tensions of the day slowly slip away, you'll begin to feel relaxed.
And then the world will seem a nicer place.

ORIGINAL AMBER
COUNTRY HERBS
LEMON BLOSSOM
Choose your fragrance to match your mood.

Plate 31   Pears
Woman *August 1977*

An advert for a painkiller (*McCalls*, April 1982)[2] portrays a woman in her late thirties in her managerial-type office. Her desk is loaded with dossiers, papers and notes, a cup of coffee, an apple and a half-eaten cup of yoghurt. Her tense facial expression and her hand touching her temple immediately tell us that she is under a tremendous strain, walking the tightrope between a job of great responsibility and a commitment to her family (represented in the private photos behind her on the wall): 'Life seems tougher when you're raising a family and working, too. Sometimes the pressure can give you a terrible headache.'

This advert faces the situation which resulted when women accepted the obligations of wage labour outside the home without having the burden of their domestic duties significantly reduced (cf. above pp. 79-81). By urging women to rely on the 'extra-strength pain reliever' to help solve the problem, the advertisement offers a solution which will remove a symptom rather than create an awareness of the factors ultimately responsible for the psychic tension, such as the husband's reluctance to assume an equal part in running the home and raising the family.

The symptom-relieving solution can also be seen in a Yeast-Vite advert where the problem is noise: 'There's one thing we all have to live with — and that's noise.' Although women frequently 'feel that vague sense of oppression' as a consequence of exposure to noise, there is nothing they can do to get rid of it: 'Nowadays the pace of life seems to include unavoidable noise that's almost never-ending.' In case the reader should attribute the noise-headache problem to a hectic urban lifestyle, she is gently reminded that noise is a universal, almost natural problem: 'Even lucky people who live in the country have to put up with tractors nowadays!' Fortunately, there's one thing you can do: 'At the first sight of pain...take out your Yeast-Vite.'

The three adverts analysed in this section, and numerous others, can be seen as indicators that the present conditions of everyday life are felt as difficult and draining. The commodity, be it pain-reliever or foam bath, functions as a kind of sedative.

Distrust of capitalist production

The following adverts can only be regarded as effective persuasion if a widespread dissatisfaction with certain aspects of capitalist production exists among the consumers, for instance with the *profit motive*. All capitalists, and probably most consumers, would accept the necessity of a certain profit margin in order to keep the investors interested in investing and to keep the wheels turning. But no manufacturer likes to be associated with the 'greedy capitalist' image; therefore, many adverts endeavour to create a distance between profits and supposedly more respectable aims like quality, the public good, and so on. The construction of an almost charitable image is the sole purpose of the so-called prestige or goodwill advertising (cf. above pp. 1-2), but also adverts within the category of commercial consumer advertising sometimes reveal that the threshold between acceptable and lavish profits is a low one in the consumers' consciousness.

An example is provided by a Stella Artois advert. On the one hand it persuades through flattery: the consumer's prosperity and discrimination are such that he 'wouldn't settle for less' than the quality of Stella Artois. But more importantly in this connection, the advert also persuades by describing the brewery's objectives as atypical: 'We brew Stella Artois as if money's no object.' Through the conjunction 'as if' this sentence manages to express that of course money is the object, but it is not the ultimate aim; the sentence therefore buttresses the brewery's image of quality by dissociating the brewing process from such an unworthy concern as money making: The more a company is driven by the profit motive, the more will it compete through price reductions and the more will the quality of the products suffer in terms of cheap raw materials and hurried production. This advertisement only makes sense if the consumer already thinks that one-sided profitability and quality are incompatible.

Similarly, many adverts testify to the fact that mass production and quality are widely regarded as incompatible. Probably no one would maintain that such incompatibility is absolute, but the verbal and visual strategies of the following adverts establish beyond any doubt a distrust of mass production in its present form.

For instance an advert for Frye Boots (*Penthouse*, September 1980) pronounces quite a severe judgment on the rest of capitalist industry if one reflects on the implications of the following body copy: 'Our men's boots are bench-crafted by skilled hands. They aren't rolled off the machine assembly line. [. . .] We're proud of the personal attention we give to details. In fact, at Frye, personal pride in the finished product is the rule, not the exception.'

For advertisers there seem to be two ways of countering the popular distruct of mass-produced commodities. If he has the slightest chance of claiming that the product is not really mass-produced this is the best strategy. In addition to the Frye Boots example we can have a look at Farmhouse Cheese (plate 32), which exploits the consumers' dissatisfaction by picturing an idyll of small-scale manufacture: this cheese 'comes from farms like Mulberry Farm, West Pennard. [. . .] Using the skills and recipes handed down over generations.' In the middle of nostalgic images of 'the rolling pastures of Cheshire' and the cows of 'local herds like John Green's Friesians', however, one cannot help wondering whether the cheese was also prepacked 'right there on the farm'? Other examples of the genuine craftmanship strategy can be seen in phrases like 'furniture . . . built with care in our family workshops in the Cotswolds' (*Sunday Times Magazine*, July 1977) and '[our] shoes are hand cut and hand fashioned', supplemented by a picture of the shoes surrounded by century-old tools (ibid.).

The second-best solution, which usually needs a more laborious explanation, consists in assuring the consumers that although the product is mass-produced, it doesn't suffer from the usual short-comings of such products. This strategy is used by a Birds Eye China Dragon advert (*Woman*, August 1977) which sets out to establish the authenticity of processed food by telling us a touching story of how a famous Chinese cook took 'control of the Birds Eye kitchen' and 'used the recipes he learnt from his mother', insisting that the Birds Eye meals should 'conform strictly to his mother's standards'.

In the course of the lengthy story the advert manages to mention all the usual objections to industrialized food: the vegetables are 'boiled to mush', there is 'gristle' in the pork, the rice 'a congealed goo', and so on. The effect is to make Birds Eye immune to this sort of criticism, since the advert recognizes its relevance and presents the Birds Eye way of meeting it: They listened and now provide an 'authentic China Dragon range'.

Oppressive moral conventions

The adverts commented on in the four previous sections have all been

Can you tell cheese from real cheese?

Cheese can be made almost anywhere. But <u>real</u> cheese has to be made on the farm. And happily it still is.

Real cheese comes from farms like Mulberry Farm, West Pennard.

On a handful of farms in Somerset, in the rolling pastures of Cheshire and in the dales of Lancashire, we make real cheese.

Traditional skills make Farmhouse cheese.

From the milk of our own local herds. Using the skills and recipes handed down over generations. So <u>real</u> cheese is Farmhouse cheese. Cheese with

Made from the milk of local herds like John Green's Friesians.

a <u>real</u> taste, rich and flavoursome. And that's the important difference.

<u>How can you find it?</u> Look for our jealously guarded Farmhouse English cheese mark on pre-packed or hand cut cheese. Your guarantee of real Cheddar, Cheshire, Lancashire & Blue Cheshire. Made right there on the farm.

FARMHOUSE English Cheese
REGISTERED

Real cheese made on the farm. By the men who produce the milk.

For further facts on real cheese, write to the Farmhouse Cheese Information Service, 26 Daleham Gardens, London NW3 5DA.

Plate 32   Farmhouse Cheese
Woman *October 1977*

concerned with the grave problems facing modern society, offering their assistance to our heroic attempts to cope with a confused and hectic everyday life. These adverts all fall into the *problem-perceptive* category, i.e. they express a 'genuine' concern with the worries and fears of ordinary people.

In this section we shall have a look at another category of advert which is also indicative of the shortcomings of the present social order, but in a different manner. This might be called the *norm-transcending* type. This category clearly indicates that the present moral and behavioural norms are experienced as unpleasant impositions which constrict our urges and desires; but they channel emancipation through the consumption of a specific commodity, and this drastically curtails the radicality of the Utopian desires.

In an advert for MG sports cars it is the commitments of married life which are seen as cumbersome, for instance in the repeated characterizations in the caption, contrasting with the fun and freedom of the picture. (plate 33).

The advert addresses bachelors, since the caption presupposes that at the moment of reading you haven't settled down. Traditional family life is seen as boring, too 'nice' and 'sensible', just like the woman you marry. In contrast, the 'MG days' which 'don't last forever' are dominated by the fun of speed, adventure and sex ('Who needs a charabanc for what you have in mind?'), and the girl in the passenger seat is supposedly anything but nice and sensible.

But in spite of the fact that it voices a serious criticism of the family, the MG advert nevertheless presents this social institution as the inevitable terminus in a man's life. 'Meantime' the MG will provide an outlet for the bachelor's recklessness which will have to be pent up when marital commitments begin 'to slow you up'. Far from challenging the normality of married life, the advert develops its gloomy prospects in order to make the ownership of an MG appear even more necessary for the optimal thrill of your bachelor days.

Rebellion against sexual norms and practices forms the main attraction point of a shoe advert (plate 34). Here the erotic frustrations and sexual inhibitions explode into a kind of riotous orgy, and the suggestiveness of the picture is supplemented by the erotic undertones of such phrases as 'red hot', 'what you fancy', 'you want it'. The evident difficulty of establishing a causal link between shoes

Someday you'll settle down with a nice, sensible girl, a nice, sensible house and a nice, sensible family saloon. Some day.

Meantime, let your hair down, put your hood down and push your foot down.

After all, you've no commitments to slow you up.

Meantime, feel the sun on your face and the wind whistling past your ears. Play tunes on the gearbox through the country backroads.

True, there are only two seats. Who needs a charabanc for what you have in mind? Meantime, just have fun. Your MG days don't last forever.

From Leyland Cars. With Supercover.

Plate 33   MG
Mayfair *August 1977*

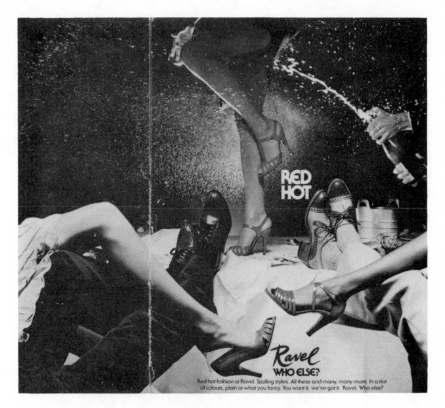

Plate 34   Ravel Shoes
She *April 1977*

and this fantasy leaves us with the possibility that the advert is simply
meant to tantalize the consumers' desires, thereby creating around
this brand of shoe an exciting erotic aura which will prove decisive
in the shoe shop.

A similar advert for Ted Lapidus Vu perfume (plate 35) draws
on the same sexual frustrations, exploiting the readers' fascination
for inventive erotic behaviour by promising to have created a
perfume 'to embrace *every little part of you*' and an '*all-embracing
heady* fragrance *who* loves you *all over*' (our italics). It is the purpose of the advert to transform its verbal aphrodisiac into the
commercial act of buying, as opposed to the sexual act of exploring
every little part of your partner.

Plate 35   Vu
Cosmopolitan *July 1977*

CONCLUSION

The advert dealt with in the previous sections only make sense against a background of popular concern with certain isolated aspects of the capitalist social order. A number of adverts, however, bear witness to more general reservations about the future of the western consumer culture. Even though a shampoo advert is talking specifically about hair, it doesn't appear unreasonable to extend its diagnosis to health as such: 'In today's world your hair is constantly under attack. Heated rollers, central heating, dirt, pollution, ill health, even the food you eat. All of them can damage your hair' (*Woman*, August 1977).

Let us for a moment, perhaps somewhat controversially, pursue the analogy between hair and human mental and physical health in general. A hair conditioner advert indirectly criticizes the norms of modern hair care: 'your hair's been coloured, permed, blown and teased to the breaking point' (*Cosmopolitan*, July 1977); so it's not unusual to have 'damaged hair'. Nevertheless, the assistance offered by the product helps you to compensate for the disadvantages of modern hair care, without you having to give up the benefits of being fashionable and glamorous.

This advert thus illustrates the spiral of problems solved and created by modern products: you wash your hair so often (daily?) that it begins to suffer; to compensate you start using conditioner which 'restores the hair's natural strength', which is broken down because you heat-dry it; to compensate, you start using a special heat-conditioner to 'keep your hair strong and supple', and so on. Who would gain, and who would suffer, if you accustomed your hair to being washed once or twice a week and let it dry by itself?

So much for hair products. It now remains to be considered whether advertising's diagnosis of and remedies for hair problems can be seen as symptomatic of the more general cultural function of advertising.

Adverts carry many indications that the hygiene and beauty products which we apply to our hair, skin, indeed our whole bodies, are damaging; the way we dress is often unhealthy; the food we eat is impoverished, lacking in fibres and vitamins; on the whole, a large part of the entire environment is unhealthy and dangerous.

Nevertheless, adverts tirelessly offer us solutions which treat the basic causes of these problems as inevitable, solutions which invite us to overcome problems through bought commodities — and individually: this is symbolically expressed in an advert for Honda commuter bikes (*Sunday Times Magazine*, July 1977) which favours the individualist solution to transport problems by picturing three swift mopeds overtaking the collective transport double-decker bus, crawling along at a snail's pace.

Possibly, the increasing frequency of adverts which mention the hazards of modern civilization can be interpreted as reflecting a growing awareness of the need to come to grips with the structural causes. The fundamental solutions sought might comprise an extension of the present boundaries of democracy towards the control of the use of human and material resources, which is now the privilege of the captains of industry.

The humble beginnings of such a demand for a widening democracy may be represented by the growing movements in Europe and the USA (e.g. the so-called 'green parties' in Germany, France and Sweden) which are motivated by a fear that the huge *productive* powers of capitalism are reaching a point where their continued exemption from public control is threatening to turn them into enormous *destructive* powers.

Meanwhile, on the micro level, advertising is offering us new commodities to make up for the harmful effects of a previous generation of commodities. On the macro level, it is doing its best to convince us that it is possible to solve the problems created by the capitalist socio-economic structure by means of the miraculous remedies developed and marketed by the individual enterprises of this structure.

6

The Ideology of Advertising

INTRODUCTION

Consider an advertisement for a hair conditioner. This advert starts off by canonizing a type of behaviour — blow-drying — which is admittedly harmful to your hair — but desirable because useful. It then goes on to present its solution to the problem: the commodity, which is supported by references to its reliance on another well-known victim of overheating, the cactus, extracts of which are among the ingredients of this product.

In other words, while the advert chooses to ignore the basic causes of the problem of overheated hair and its possible damaging longterm effects, using heated hair appliances is presented as the only normal thing to do. And any reader who might have got worried after reading the horror story about weak and brittle hair is rapidly and authoritatively brought back to the herd of blow-dryer loyalists: she is reminded that, obviously, she won't want to give up using a blow-dryer.

Adverts which state their desired behavioural norms as openly as the one mentioned are relatively infrequent. It is much more usual for adverts to take a certain *behavioural normalcy* for granted as if incontestable. An advert for foot deodorants (*Cosmopolitan*, July 1977) labours to establish as necessary and normal the use of foot deodorants. The method is to draw a historical parallel to underarm deodorants, which are thus taken as an unquestionable necessity: 'There was a time when no one used an underarm deodorant either.' The advert is therefore trying to evoke and to exploit people's disgust at the mere thought of the days when people smelled like people under the arms, in order to make them equally disgusted with the natural smell of their feet, thus alienating them from their own body sensations.

Admittedly, sweaty feet can be quite nasty, and the advert actually mentions the causes of the problem: 'Shoes made of synthetic materials, so your feet can't breathe. And tights and tight boots, which don't help either.' It therefore requires a considerable amount of impudence to continue with a sentence which suggests that the solution lies not in the abolition of the causes but in the use of yet another commodity: '*So* not surprisingly, a good few people have already discovered the solution. [X] Foot-Deodorant.' (our italics).

In addition to illustrating the phenomenon of implied behavioural normalcy, this advert thus provides a clear example of *problem reduction*: Instead of solving the problem of smelly feet through non-suffocating alternatives to your present foot and leg wear, the advert offers a product which helps you to offset the undesirable side-effects of following unhealthy fashions, while increasing your dependence on bought products.

Indeed, both mechanisms are essential for advertising's endeavour to persuade readers that needs can be fulfilled and problems solved through consumption. The mechanisms are extremely frequent in adverts for sanitary protection. The problem situation confronted by these adverts at the outset is the monthly period; the objective is to create confidence, and the solution is Simplicity, Lil-lets, or whatever. But in order to solve the problem, it is necessary for sanitary protection adverts to reduce a complex phenomenon, consisting of physical, psychological and emotional elements, to being solely a matter of bodily excretions. All sanitary protection aids can solve this problem through their 'maximum absorbency' and 'leak-proof lining'; and the confidence resulting from the 'total protection' is then shown to solve all other monthly recurring problems: the women are pictured as happy and carefree, moving with panache; their vitality almost appears to reach a monthly peak which enables them to be perfect company for husband, children and friends, and to be as competent and creative as ever on the job (see the 'Simplicity' and 'Tampax' adverts, plates 12 and 18). Only by ignoring the multifaceted character of the period problem can advertisements succeed in constructing so idealized images of femininity that they can hope to conquer a larger share of a market where product loyalty remains great.

These idealized images have the further effect of conditioning women to suppress the pain, the fears and depressions which frequently accompany periods; in other words, these images create a normalcy of behaviour and values around periods which urges individual women to conceal a natural body function. At the same time they strengthen the social taboo on menstruation.

Some adverts are quite explicit about it, reassuring women that 'they don't show, even under close-fitting clothes' (*Cosmopolitan*, July 1977). Others are more subtle, and more dangerous from an ideological point of view, because the norm they propagate remains on a latent, 'natural' level, which means that the reader accepts the norm as unquestionable without subjecting it to conscious rational scrutiny.

The headline of an advert for Dr White's Panty Pads (*Woman*, July 1977) asks 'Is there anything you can't wear?' Since the question doesn't strike one as meaningless, it must imply that with other towels there *are* things you can't wear. And it relies on the reader to supply the causal connection: because other towels are *visible*. Through its use of verbal expectation (cf. pp. 24-7) it reinforces the behavioural rule that periods are something which a woman should keep secret, even to herself: 'Even you won't know you're wearing them.' This provides the ideal background for offering the female reader a means of observing the rule.

Before we go on to discuss ideology in more general terms, it might be helpful to illustrate the phenomena of problem reduction and behavioural normality as they occur in an advert for Londun Line curl remover in the Black South African *Drum Magazine* (plate 36). The different political and cultural environment of the Londun Line advert may be sufficiently unfamiliar to European readers to make the effects of the two mechanisms stand out more clearly.

The black woman pictured in the advert has the problem of being black in a white-dominated apartheid society. This problem is then reduced from being a political and social one to the cosmetic problem of straight vs. curly hair, which is a great deal easier to solve — although it means a complete negation of her indigenous characteristics and a first step towards the acceptance of white appearance and behaviour. The logic of the advert implies that the solution to the underprivileged position of Black people does not consist in struggling for racial equality, but in ceasing to be Black. If the

Plate 36   Londun Line
Drum Magazine *October 1981*

transformation between 'before' and the smiling 'after treatment' is anything to go by, it has been worth her while — and less dangerous than joining the political struggle for racial equality.

We regard the semantic processes of problem reduction and imposition of a behavioural normalcy as the most general ideological mechanisms of advertising, since by ideology we wish to understand those structures of meaning which misrepresent phenomena, states and processes in our culture; or which assert or presuppose the naturalness and inevitability of such phenomena, states and processes.[1]

IDEOLOGY

For the purposes of this book, the really insidious ideological processes are those which treat a phenomenon as so self-evident and natural as to exempt it completely from critical inspection and to render it inevitable; those beliefs which remain unquestioned because they are represented as unquestionable; those messages which, being surrounded by an aura of pure 'common sense', do not simply try to arrest or reverse on-going social change, but presuppose that such change is impossible.

In order to demonstrate that ideological attitudes are not simply synonymous with 'reactionary misapprehensions', we may consider an ideological belief which is still widely shared across the political spectrum and commercially exploited in the brand name Mothercare: the idea that maternal love is natural. If we break the spell of this ideology and say that a mother's love of her child is not natural, most people will probably contradict us.

This reaction can partly be explained linguistically by the fact that 'the natural' has come to assume such high esteem that to say that something or somebody is not natural amounts to saying that it or he/she is abnormal. However, the reaction also reflects the inbred belief that the ties between mother and child are so strong that nothing can sever them and that the difference between maternal and paternal love is one of kind, not degree.

Nevertheless, historians and anthropologists (for instance the French historian and philosopher Elisabeth Badinter in her book *L'amour en plus* (1980) have established that maternal love is merely one 'option' for the woman who has given birth to a child, and that the choice of this option is determined by social and historical circumstances rather than by transhistorical features of the female psyche. In our society the ideology of maternal love can be regarded as a buttress for a traditional family structure and an economically dependent woman's access to self-respect. Today, some men might regard the sacred maternal ties as a female prerogative in which they would like to have a share.

This example may serve to illustrate the common-sense status of ideology, and the concept of common sense in turn enables us to grasp the essence of ideology as being simultaneously that which is openly available for all to see and that which is invisible because of its obviousness.

We recognize, therefore, that 'ideology' is a necessary component of human life: if we did not cling to certain fundamental attitudes and ways of thinking, our consciousness would be in a total flux which would paralyse us completely. Nevertheless, we have to realize that even our fundamental values are products of human cognition and cultural processes, and as such are subject to change.

The ideology of advertising is harmful because it reinforces those tendencies which seek to make society static; not in the sense of avoiding the development of new products and the construction of more leisure facilities, but in the sense of retarding or preventing the revision of the basic principles of the social order both at the macro ('democracy') and micro (sex roles) levels.

Market Consciousness

One of the most striking ideological aspects about the world portrayed in adverts is the almost total absence of work. We have attributed this absence to the day-dream character of much advertising, interpreting it symbolically as reflecting widespread discontent with the industrial work process (cf. pp. 131-3).

By ignoring practically all phenomena to do with production, advertising undoubtedly serves the escapist need of its readers, while also serving its own interest in concealing the fundamental inequality in the sphere of production (cf. p. 7). The resulting *market consciousness* is one of the most general and salient features of the dominant ideology. It appears for instance in the way in which advertising only concerns itself with products once they have appeared on the market; the labour process in which the raw material is manufactured by means of machinery and human labour is ignored. It is thereby taken for granted that the current mode of social labour organization is unquestionable and inevitable; we need only concern ourselves with its results, while the circumstances of the process are irrelevant.

Alternatively, production is pictured in hopelessly nostalgic or romanticized terms which bear little resemblance to production in advanced industrial society. Let us return to the advert for Farmhouse cheese (plate 32) for a concrete example of the nostalgia surrounding the production of food. The advert does show a manufacturing link between cow and cheese, but a very old-fashioned and rural one, without any trace of the modern machinery which was used, presumably not only to 'prepack' but also to produce the cheese. Apparently, in spite of the many obvious advantages of technologized production, it is always painful for manufacturers to be reminded of the drawbacks of mass production: the associations of cheap, low-quality products, and the inevitable regimentation and alienation of a work-force sometimes having to work in three shifts — in order to recover the enormous expenditure of acquiring the machinery — irrespective of the disintegrating effects on family life.

Appart from such excursions to idyllic small-scale places of manufacture, the universal market consciousness of advertising obscures the real relations of the social order, by representing 'a system which requires both production and exchange, as if it consisted of exchange only, [. . .] we can no longer "see" that it is in production that labour is exploited and the surplus value extracted' (Hall 1977: 323).

Keeping within the limits of the market means that the antagonistic foundations of capitalist society are masked and concealed, for it is only in the market that the basic, supposedly inalienable rights of freedom and equality have any practical validity (cf. pp. 7-8).

Moreover, the lack of fully democratic freedom and equality in the far-reaching decisions of the economy is compensated for by the freedom of choice on the market which plays an important part in many advertisements. Advertising thus has another important social function:

The fact that this function has not been planned as a purpose by those who make and use publicity in no way lessens its significance. Publicity turns consumption into a substitute for democracy. The choice of what one eats (or wears or drives) takes the place of significant political choice. Publicity helps to mask and compensate for all that is undemocratic within society.

(Berger 1972:149)

The function described by Berger can be observed in the role of advertising as an institution whose very visibility in society comes to symbolize freedom of choice, free enterprise, and ultimately the 'Free World'. It also surfaces in individual adverts; a kitchen advert, for instance, openly exploits the ideology of freedom through consumption: Moffat gas kitchens 'give you complete freedom and flexibility in planning your kitchen', even the oven liners are called 'Freedom', 'You choose' where you want it, they 'give you a tremendous choice', and so on (*Woman*, October 1977). Another example is provided by an advert for Buf-Puf pimple sponges which significantly places the information that 'America loves Buf-Puf and so will you' in a speech balloon attached to a miniature goddess of Liberty inserted into the bottom of the picture (*Cosmopolitan*, July 1977).

Individuals and Groups

In chapter 4 we noted how the persuasive strategy of a number of adverts, especially those addressed to a middle-class audience, relies on a fairly strong emphasis on individualism, as when an advert for Miners cosmetics assures you that with their eye crayons you'll get 'a bit more individual' (ibid.), and when Kotex Brevia pant-liners are said to be intended 'specially for every woman who's ever had to cope with vaginal discharge' (*Woman*, August 1977).

Although the body copy of the advert says explicitly that vaginal discharge can occur for any woman at any time, the way in which each reader is addressed attempts to make her *feel* she's something special. In this way, the advertiser makes the appeal of the product simultaneously all-inclusive and uniquely personal.

Similarly, when a photo equipment advert says that 'without it you'll never know how good you are' (*Sunday Times Magazine*,

July 1977) it attributes to us, the readers, a great potential for photography, while stressing that only a particular make will do our talents justice. The individualism presupposed by these adverts originates in the market consciousness discussed in the previous section and is in fact one of its structural corollaries. For although capitalist industrial production, because of its dynamic, expansive development, comes to depend more and more on an increasing division and interdependence of labour, this tendency towards interdependence is counteracted in the sphere of circulation: in a capitalist system our consciousness of the exchange of commodities in the market is distorted, so that what is basically a social transaction between interdependent parties (cf. above pp. 7-8) appears as an individual relation between mutually indifferent buyers and sellers, and so that 'the common good' is conceived of as automatically derived from each individual's pursuit of his own happiness.[2]

Whenever this individualism is exploited in adverts, it has the effect of keeping individuals apart by confirming us in our precious uniqueness, providing us with 'imaginary blinkers in preventing us from looking sideways and recognizing other people, contiguous to us' (Williamson 1978: 54) and thus persuading all of us to express our particular uniqueness by means of the same mass-produced product. But when the possession and use of a certain commodity becomes sufficiently prestigious, the producer will often profit by abandoning individualizing flattery and instead emphasizing the consumers' 'communal ownership' and use of the commodity and the lifestyle surrounding it. After having fragmented the classes of modern society into unique individuals, advertising thus goes on to impose an imaginary coherence on the fragmented units through consumer groups, as seen in such phrases as '*Stresstabs people* take it to the limit' (*Runner's World*, August 1982) (our emphasis).

This imaginary coherence may have very unfortunate consequences because it sets up

a particular formation of groups which cannot be mistaken for the groups of class difference. Advertisements obscure and avoid the real issues of society, those relating to work: to jobs and wages and who works for whom. They create systems of social differentiation which are a veneer on the basic class structure of our society.

(Williamson 1978: 47)

Before we leave these general aspects of advertising ideology, we shall consider an advert for Whitbread (plate 37) which illustrates some of the phenomena just dealt with. This falls within the category of prestige or goodwill advertising since its objective is to create long-term goodwill with the public rather than harvesting an immediate increase in sales. It is a follow-up to a previous advert which raised the questions of licensing hours and which is reprinted as part of the advert under consideration.

Right from the beginning, this advert is aiming to build an image of working for the common good. By referring to questionnaire sociology it invokes society's processes of political opinion-formation and decision-making. This becomes more explicit towards the end where the efforts of the brewery are placed in the context of 'Parliament' and 'the Judiciary': quite obviously Whitbread are engaged in a democratic struggle for civil rights, namely the right to drink beer in a pub at any time you wish. In other words, Whitbread are promoting their ultimate interest in selling more beer by invoking our most precious political mechanism — parliamentary democracy — while keeping this interest in the background (cf. our analysis of the Stella Artois advert p. 132).

At no point do they state that commercial goals induced them to start this campaign, or that they are hoping to increase their sales. On the contrary, they present themselves as being driven by worthy temperance motives, quoting one correspondent as saying that increasing opening hours 'would have the effect of lessening the amount of drunkenness'.

The location of Whitbread within the parliamentary framework is supported by their faithfulness to the principles of social science: they are concerned with reliable opinion surveys, they do not jump to conclusions on the basis of an unrepresentative group of regular pub-goers. And the fact that their interests remain in the dark contributes to the impression that they are actuated by nothing but considerations of public welfare, giving voice to the unfortunate, inarticulate group of pub customers: 'Our customers don't have an articulate lobby.'

In operating with this type of social grouping, Whitbread are cutting across the basic social categories of class, substituting groups 'organized' around products (in this case beer). This consumer sociology is tied up with political sociology in that pub customers

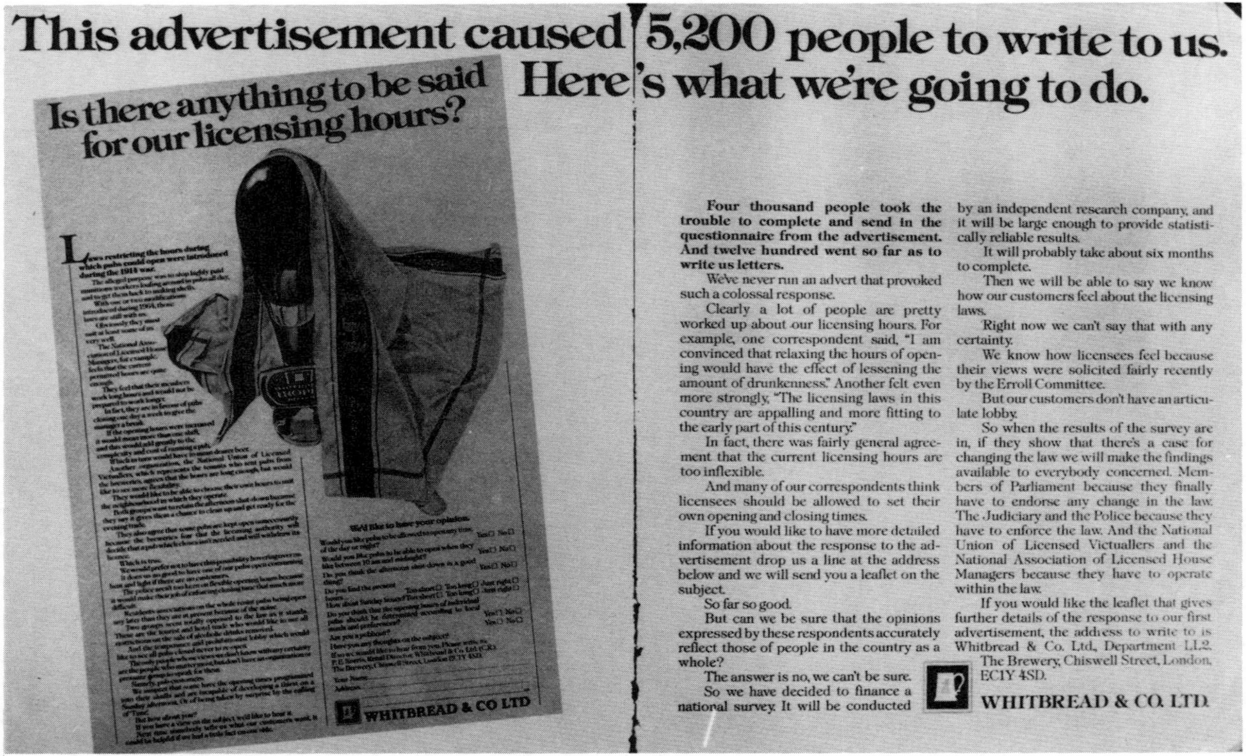

This is an advertisement reproduced as a plate. The advertisement reads:

This advertisement caused 5,200 people to write to us. Here's what we're going to do.

Is there anything to be said for our licensing hours?

Four thousand people took the trouble to complete and send in the questionnaire from the advertisement. And twelve hundred went so far as to write us letters.

We've never run an advert that provoked such a colossal response.

Clearly a lot of people are pretty worked up about our licensing hours. For example, one correspondent said, "I am convinced that relaxing the hours of opening would have the effect of lessening the amount of drunkenness." Another felt even more strongly. "The licensing laws in this country are appalling and more fitting to the early part of this century."

In fact, there was fairly general agreement that the current licensing hours are too inflexible.

And many of our correspondents think licensees should be allowed to set their own opening and closing times.

If you would like to have more detailed information about the response to the advertisement drop us a line at the address below and we will send you a leaflet on the subject.

So far so good.

But can we be sure that the opinions expressed by these respondents accurately reflect those of people in the country as a whole?

The answer is no, we can't be sure.

So we have decided to finance a national survey. It will be conducted by an independent research company, and it will be large enough to provide statistically reliable results.

It will probably take about six months to complete.

Then we will be able to say we know how our customers feel about the licensing laws.

Right now we can't say that with any certainty.

We know how licensees feel because their views were solicited fairly recently by the Errol Committee.

But our customers don't have an articulate lobby.

So when the results of the survey are in, if they show that there's a case for changing the law we will make the findings available to everybody concerned. Members of Parliament because they finally have to endorse any change in the law. The Judiciary and the Police because they have to enforce the law. And the National Union of Licensed Victuallers and the National Association of Licensed House Managers because they have to operate within the law.

If you would like the leaflet that gives further details of the response to our first advertisement, or the address to write to is Whitbread & Co. Ltd, Department L12, The Brewery, Chiswell Street, London, EC1Y 4SD.

WHITBREAD & CO LTD

Plate 37 Whitbread
Sunday Times Magazine July 1977

are claimed to be a pressure group which is as yet still unorganized.

The absurdity of this idea becomes clear if we take it to its logical conclusion: a society where people are attached to political pressure groups related to each commodity they buy. It goes without saying that such groups would have quite contradictory aims, as is indeed the case in this advert: Mr Smith as a member of a residents' association is against longer opening hours 'because of the noise', but as a pub customer Mr Smith is allegedly in favour of less restriction on pub hours. Which interest is to overrule the other? This advert clearly implies the latter, and in the process misrepresents the social categories of class.

SPECIFIC IDEOLOGIES OF ADVERTISING

Meaning transfer in advertisements[3]

The ideological market consciousness and its derived sub-ideologies are extremely common in advertising, although they rarely appear at the manifest level of persuasion, i.e. as a meaning complex referred to by a concrete advert in order to give the commodity a symbolic value or 'image'.

This role is played by such meaning complexes as history, nature, science and others, which are already established as ideological systems prior to their adoption by adverts. Following Williamson (1978: 99 ff.), we shall term these ideological systems referred to be advertisements 'referent systems'.

We regard them as 'ideological' because they mediate currently dominant attitudes to history, nature, and so on, as if they were universally true and valid (cf. p. 145). However, they should be seen as ideological complexes which belong on a different level from the ideologies connected with the market consciousness. The latter are not just 'a descriptive feature of capitalism . . . [They] perform a pivotal role in the maintenance of capitalist relations' (Hall 1977: 331), while the former are more 'accidental' ideological phenomena. For instance, the current practices and norms of gender behaviour are not structurally given in the capitalist mode of production, and the regressive distortion by advertising of real gender behaviour is not a structural necessity for capitalism, however expedient it is for patriarchy. This means that the specific referent systems used by adverts are never static; they continuously change along with changes in social practices and attitudes.

The symbolic meaning possessed by a given referent system is subjected to two processes of meaning-transmission in advertisements. In practice the two processes are simultaneous, but analytically we have to separate them and take them one after the other.

Usually the advertiser wants to give his product an image, intended to function as an extra asset for the product in the market where it has to be somehow differentiated from competing products which are (near-) identical in terms of material use value. The problem he faces is how to get the reader-consumer to associate the product with the desired image or quality; the solution is to picture the commodity juxtaposed with an object or person[4] whose possession of the quality is obvious to the reader; if he doesn't trust the reader to be able to make the 'irrational mental leap' (Williamson 1978: 43) which associates the 'objective correlative' and the commodity, he may provide a stimulus embedded into the formal structure of the advert, for instance its colour distribution. If it all works out, the process can be diagrammed like this:

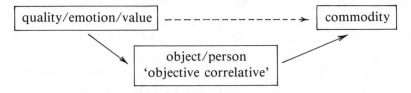

A soft-drink advert pictures the successive stages of pulling a pair of jeans up over the hips; however, you only have to read the three pictures backwards in order to see a woman pulling her jeans *down* over her hips. The close-fitting jeans in the illustrations therefore come to mean 'slimness' and 'eroticism'; these values are transferred to the commodity through the joint effects of juxtaposition and colour co-ordination: the colours of the panties and the jeans are easily associated with the trade mark colour of the soft drink.

Since the relationship established between clothes and commodity is based on visual *similarity* (colour), it falls into the category of *metaphorical* relationships; and since it is the *contiguity* in the image of clothes and commodity which makes our consciousness work to establish the similarity in the first place, we see that *metonymy* is also operative in the value transfer to the commodity (cf. pp. 38-42). Finally, this process is the one described in the first chapter by the concept 'aestheticization of commodities' (cf. pp. 8-9).

The second process of meaning transfer usually merely completes the first, by insisting or implying that the value transferred to the commodity will be transferred to the consumer through the act of buying it:

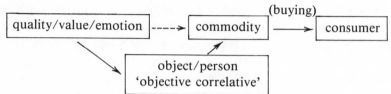

The caption of the soft drink advert demonstrates this process: by saying that you can do it the advert first presupposes that the reader *wants* to do 'it' i.e. to pull her trousers down — and up; secondly, it claims that it is through the commodity that the ideal can be attained — they can help.

An advert for French Almond fragrances (*Cosmopolitan*, July 1977) endeavours to associate the various fragrances sold under that brand name with 'Frenchness'. This quality, which is usually regarded as superior in matters pertaining to the erotic and the gastronomic, is mainly evoked verbally: the cologne is 'inspired by sheer joie de vivre', made for 'girls who admire the panache of the French'; the quality is equated with the product through the name': *French* Almond. The transfer of this enviable quality to the consumer through the act of buying is insisted on in what is almost a threat: 'Don't imagine you can do without that elusive je-ne-sais-quoi.'

Advertising, then, first *aestheticizes the commodity*, transforming it into a desirable attribute for the consumer who wants to succeed in some respect. Secondly, when this attribute has been transferred to the consumer through the purchase of the commodity, it *aestheticizes the consumer* whose veneer of glamourous commodities is supposed to appeal to the senses and desires of other people, just as the commodity is made to appeal to the senses and desires of the consumer, through the image created by advertisements.

Actually the word 'aestheticization' may not be too fortunate in connection with the meaning processes of advertising; it was originally conceived by Haug to cover the wider field of commodity cosmetics, additives, colourful wrappings, and so on, of which advertising is only a part. But important aspects of the symbolic meaning processes in adverts are not covered by it.

Literally 'aestheticize' means something like 'to please by means of sense impressions', but when we say that an advert aestheticizes the commodity, we mean more than that; we also mean that it *'ideologizes' the commodity* by placing it in an ideological context which rubs off on the commodity (for instance, the happy family, omnipotent technology, Nature). Thus the commodity is made to appeal to the consciously or subconsciously held values of the consumer. By connecting personally and socially desirable values and feelings with commodities, advertising links 'possible *un*attainable things with those that *are* attainable, and thus reassures us that the former are within reach' (Williamson 1978: 31).

This signifying process represents a reversal of the pre-capitalist state of affairs, where the cultural relationship in which people engaged endowed the products which they produced and used with certain values:

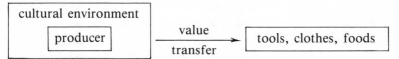

Foods, clothes and tools symbolically expressed the people who had produced or used them. But now the symbolic value of a product is created in calculated campaigns and transferred to the people who buy and consume them. The symbolic value is transmitted to the consumer by the advert through the commodity, which is thus invested with magic powers while leaving the consumer inactive. The consumer, increasingly deprived of his role as a producer of useful things, is restored as a producer of symbolic effects only in so far as he accepts the consumer role. In other words, an original organic process of interaction between man and nature, resulting in the production of the means of subsistence, is superseded by an alienated process of 'manufacturing' an identity through the consumption of commodities.

We shall now have a look at two of the most common referent systems exploited by advertising — nature and history — in order to investigate the concrete manner in which these phenomena are transferred as symbolic meaning to commodities.

Nature and 'the natural'

If for a moment we suppose, for the sake of the argument, that we could look upon advertising from a position of naïve innocence, how would we expect the phenomenon of nature to appear in ads; Our innocence would probably lead us to think of nature as something lasting, as that which is not changed by the intervention of human culture, as a force which exists independently of culture; consequently, we would think of 'natural' behaviour or a 'natural' appearance as completely unspoiled and uncontrolled by human interference.

However, we would not have to expose ourselves to advertisements for very long in order to arrive at a pretty abrupt transition from naïve innocence to undeceived experience, maybe passing through a stage of growing puzzlement as we go from one advert to another.

A Mary Quant advert (*Cosmopolitan*, July 1977) offers the reader practical assistance with skin cosmetics. As you read about the gamut of skin care products which are supposedly necessary if you want to 'look your fashionable best, every minute of every day', you cannot help being slightly surpirsed that it is only *after* the application of cleanser, toner, moisturizer, foundation and powder that 'Blushbaby gives your face a natural glow'. What is 'natural' supposed to mean here?

We are somewhat reassured in our innocence, however, when reading the first sentences of an advert for Miners make-up (ibid.): 'The best looks seem to happen naturally. No pretence, no flouncy special effects.' Nevertheless, being a cosmetics advert, it has to suggest a compromise between the natural and the artifical which minimizes the role of the artificial make-up: 'A lot of you, a little of Miners...so that the final effect is just naturally you.' At this stage we are probably beginning to realize that in the universe of advertising there is no contradiction between the natural and the artificial; or rather, the signifying processes of advertisements are engaged in a ceaseless struggle to negate this contradiction, and even to convince us that 'the Natural Look' can only be achieved *through* cosmetics. Little wonder, when 'The Natural Look means trying to look as if we'd just stepped in from a country garden, after eight gruelling hours of work and a rush-hour scrum' (Miners). Still, we're left with no explanation as to *why* it is desirable always to look 'as if we'd just stepped in from a country garden'? And *why* it is essential to dissociate artificial beauty from 'pretence'?

Our last example of the gulf between the natural body and the advertising ideal of 'the natural' is an advert for eye cosmetics (*Cosmopolitan*, July 1977). It relies on the readers' liking for the illogical in order for them to accept that although the 'heavy, black eye make-up looks old-fashioned now...the natural clear-eyed look takes almost as much time to achieve.' i.e. a natural look is something to be achieved through a laborious process. As regards eyebrows, it is taken for granted that you want to pluck or wax them (at least the advert is liberal enough to give you that choice): 'After you've plucked or waxed them to the shape you want, accentuate them.' It is thus regarded as inconceivable that you might want to leave your eyebrows as nature created them.

This advert also hints that the answer to the first question above should be sought in the social role of women in a patriarchal society. Asking 'how do you stand up to such close scrutiny?' the advert clearly nourishes women's fear of being weighed and found wanting, of missing a chance of a love relationship or a job because you didn't live up to the standard.

In order to answer the second question about the cultural causes of the positive evaluation of nature and the natural, we shall have to go beyond these phenomena as they appear in advertising and consider the interrelation between nature and culture in western civilization as a whole.

'Nature is the primary referent of a culture', says Williamson (1978: 103), because a culture is nothing but nature transformed in order to fulfil the needs of men: 'If a culture is to refer to itself, therefore, it can only do so by the representation of its transformation of nature — it has meaning in terms of what it has *changed*' (ibid.). The background to the growing symbolic role of nature is the increasing distance of society from its natural 'raw material' through industrial and technological development. 'The natural' first appears as a positive value in the eighteenth century when it becomes necessary to legitimate alienated urban behaviour by invoking the relation to the sacred natural origin.

Therefore, the desire for the natural ideal can be seen as a symbolic criticism of a culture which is increasingly replacing the natural with the synthetic. Suspended between this critical consciousness and the economic need to give free rein to unbroken industrial expansion, the shared social ideal of 'the natural' embodies 'the inherent tension of a society which both ravages the natural world and violates natural human needs, yet seeks to represent its workings *as* natural, hence inviolable' (Williamson 1978: 110).

As became clear in our analyses of the three adverts in this section, 'the natural' is a concept which need not have very much, if anything, to do with nature. This is even more evident in an advert for toilet paper which claims that since they use soft toilet paper at home, 'it's only natural that people expect to find it at work' (*Sunday Times Magazine*, July 1977).

These examples all testify to a (not very recent) semantic change whereby the meaning of 'natural' has become merely that degree of approximation to nature which a historically specific cutlure defines as desirable, a 'justification for whatever society approves and desires' (Williamson 1978: 123). A one-to-one relationship is established between 'the natural' and the morally acceptable — the normal and the obvious on the one hand, and 'the unnatural' and the deviant on the other. The equation between the obvious and the natural is deliberately played upon by adverts using the adverb 'naturally'. Asserting that Schwarzkopf toning 'makes Natures' shades look best — naturally!' (*Cosmopolitan*, July 1977), an advert exploits the ambiguity of 'naturally' between a modal and a manner adverb: 'naturally' (modal), nature's shades look best, and if these shades are transferred to your hair 'naturally' (manner) there is just no way that you can become artificial in the process. When used by advertising, 'the natural' therefore becomes a mechanism which allows culture to appropriate the positive qualities associated with nature, and to attach these qualities, deprived of their substance, to industrially manufactured products.

When we analyse adverts which rely on 'the natural', it is our purpose to disentangle this ideological mechanism, in order to demonstrate how its justification of current forms of behaviour and consciousness has a conservative effect on social processes of change. As long as we accept these forms as 'natural' we shall also regard them not only as desirable but as inevitable.

The ideology of 'the natural': four variants

In adverts nature and 'the natural' occur in four variants.

1   In the first type, nature is claimed to be an *ingredient in the product*, which is given status and significance in terms of its natural raw material. This attempt to equate a natural source and a commodity is found in an advert which boasts that 'only natural ingredients give Blue Band its light taste' (*Cosmopolitan*, July 1977); and in another example from 1982 which recommends creme rinses which 'bring back the bounce and lustre that modern living tends to knock out of your hair. And they do it with pure natural ingredients'.

Most foods and many cosmetics fall into this category, where the essence of nature is so to speak encapsulated in the product. In a few extreme cases the equation between raw material and commodity seems justified, for instance an advert for Perrier table water can legitimately claim that the product is pure nature: 'He added nothing and took nothing away', it is 'a precious gift of Nature' which 'springs naturally to mind' (*Cosmopolitan*, July 1977). The same can be said of Cerebos Salt where human intervention in the 'production process' is minimal: 'The sea gathers it. The sun dries it' (*Sunday Times Magazine*, July 1977).

2   Many adverts present their commodities as *improvements on nature*, i.e. as somehow superior to their natural source. When the advert in question is for cosmetics, it may offer to lend (human) nature a hand. Thus, one which promises that its hair dye will only 'make more of what nature gave you' is based on the assumption that deep down we're all naturally perfect — we just need the product as a catalyst to bring it out.

Other beauty adverts in this category rest on the assumption that nature makes no one perfect; perfect beauty can only be achieved through the use of cosmetics, which are necessary since it is vital for a woman to make others *believe* that she is naturally beautiful, and hence enviable:

'We're none of us perfect,' says Mary Quant.
'Let's face it, most of us would like to improve on nature a little. Especially if we thought we could get away with it without anyone noticing.'

3   A number of adverts actually *counteract natural processes* in the name of 'the natural'. This is illustrated in an advert for hair colour for men, which claims to be able to restore your hair's 'natural, youthful look', thereby implying that greying hair is not natural — which it isn't, of course, if 'natural' is taken to be synonymous with 'desirable' or 'prestigious'.

In this category we also find adverts for clothes whose primary use value is a moral rather than a material matter, for instance bathing suits and bras. The discrepancy between nature and 'the natural' is made exceptionally clear by an example cited by Williamson: the caption of a bra advert saying that when you wear it you 'look very natural, but not naked' (Williamson 1978: 121).

Most sanitary protection adverts belong in this category too in so far as they attempt to connect the effect of their product with 'the natural'. The Tampax girl (plate 38) finds herself in a pretty awkward situation, struggling against an external wilderness-nature; however, her situation is made less awkward because she is assisted by Tampax in her struggle with her internal nature.

4   In the last category we find adverts which try to sell products without the faintest connection to Nature by *imposing Nature as a referent system*. A Peugeot advert (*Cosmopolitan*, July 1977) illustrates this category: a car is placed in a beautiful wild scenery, a romantic image of nature intended to be vaguely associated with the car, presumably merging with the values connoted by the lion symbol used by Peugeot.

At this point it is necessary to stress that the four categories are not mutually exclusive; their uses of nature may be simultaneously present in adverts, as is the case with 'Nature's Riches' (ibid.) whose four varieties of conditioner are 'enriched by Avocado Cream', 'caressed by Strawberry Shine', and so on (category 1); at the same time the conditioners 'improve your hair', 'restoring its own softness' (category 2).

It must also be emphasized that it is not 'the same' nature which is referred to throughout. In some cases the nature which is exploited is human physical nature (categories 2 and 3), in others it is authentic 'wild' nature (categories 1 and 4), and in yet others it is cultivated nature in the shape of gardens and fields which is invoked (categories 1, 2 and 4).

Plate 38   Tampax
Cosmopolitan October 1981

History

Faced with an advert for Camel cigarettes (*Penthouse*, September 1980), you may ask yourself what a brand of cigarettes could possibly have to do with the Sphinx? Ordinarily, of course, you wouldn't ask such a question, being so familiar with commodities juxtaposed with baffling objects and scenes. But since we are here concerned with meaning processes of advertising, we have to defamiliarize ourselves with what may appear quite straightforward at a first glance.

We are simply witnessing another example of value transfer (cf. pp. 152-6). The associations evoked by the quite arbitrary brand name Camel and the yellow-orange pyramid on the packet provide the connection with the Middle East and ancient Egypt, which is reinforced by the yellow-orange sky behind the Sphinx. For the benefit of slow-witted readers of the advert, a camel silhouette stands out against the sky, making clear the Camel/camel → desert → Egypt connection. The advert also exploits the myth of the solution of the Sphinx's riddle by claiming that Camel has 'solved' the problem of creating 'taste in low tar', which is probably quite a riddle to some smokers.

The Camel advert exemplifies the most basic way in which history is exploited in commercial messages: because the present is experienced as insufficient, adverts project images of a mythical and imprecise history to lend cultural authority to commodities.

A second way in which history is exploited ideologically appears in an advert for a skin cream, which recommends the product through a historical reference: Ancient Egyptians discovered the moisturising properties of a certain plant, supposed to treat the effects of the sun and wind on the skin. Most people living in today's urban environment are rarely exposed to the damaging effects of the alleged origin. Consequently, the causes of their skin problems must be found in today's environment which supposedly includes industrial as well as cosmetic pollution. By ignoring these causes and only mentioning the natural exposure of ancient Egyptians, the historical reference diminishes the urgency of contemporary (skin) problems by attributing them to timeless, universal causes.

Adverts also use history in a more subtle manner. The advert for Pyrex casseroles (plate 27), drawing on working-class language, humorously exploits the readers' knowledge of the upstairs-downstairs relationship, but empties this knowledge of historical content by placing the product as the historical cause of the disappearance of servants: 'with casseroles in clear glass, and beautifully designed decorative casseroles, upstairs people became more than willing to cook and serve for themselves.' The Pyrex advert thus exemplifies the use of history as a 'reference system', a meaning complex referred to without its substance, the empty shell being used to give status to the product.

Since it is addressed to 'Ethel's' descendants, the advert also has implications for class consciousness: the reader's female ancestors were not among the people who had life made simple for them by 'Ethels' until they became more 'willing' to cook for themselves after the invention of Pyrex. Nevertheless, these are the people whom the working-class reader is asked to identify with and to copy. Having earned her mistress's approval, Pyrex now offers itself to 'Ethel'.

No one can miss the humour in this advert, for instance in the concluding paragraph beginning 'If your servants have left' and in the startling equation of a human being with a kitchen utensil: 'Before Pyrex casseroles, there was something almost as useful called Ethel. If you owned an Ethel...' The question now arises whether the distortion of history is softened by these humorous passages? While this is certainly a matter of discussion, we believe that this is not the case. Especially since the joke is clearly on the downstairs people whom history 'promoted' from servants to wage-labourers, the effect of the humour is (at best) a trivializing one.

'RECUPERATIVE' ADVERTISING

In the sections on nature and history we have seen how advertising exploits other systems of meaning as 'referent systems', reducing the natural to a synonym of the desriable, and distorting historical processes and phenomena. While stripping these meaning complexes of specific content, adverts retain a vague aura of the meaning complex in question in order to appropriate its authority and transfer it to a commodity.

Because it ignores the substance of the meanings it appropriates, advertising can draw on the most unlikely referent systems and even use 'ideas, systems, phenomena in society whose actual content and body of thought is hostile to advertising and might seem completely alien to it. But the more hostile, the better use advertising can make of it, for its recuperation from criticism then seems all the more miraculous' (Williamson 1978: 170). This *recuperative capacity* of advertising can be defined as its capacity to assimilate or neutralize hostile attitudes, its ability to regain strength after a blow *through* the blow, turning it to serve its own purposes. This capacity can be directed both towards critical attacks on social phenomena such as the class society and the suppression of women or blacks, and towards criticism of advertising itself.

Recuperating from social criticism

The Women's Lib and Black Power movements are both based on attitudes which are highly critical of, or even antagonistic to, the behavioural norms and unequal distribution of privileges in western consumer society which advertising seems to epitomize. However, that doesn't render these movements immune to exploitation in the sale strategies of advertising.

In a well-known series of cigarette adverts, a contrast is drawn between a historical situation when women couldn't smoke cigarettes and a modern, glamorous woman smoking a cigarette; in some of the adverts the woman is smiling incredulously at the thought of the restrictions of the past while the advert is reminding her that she's come a long way. This advert congratulates women for having won from men the right to smoke. By equating Women's Lib with demands like the right to smoke, it works to trivialize an important historical movement, projecting what was a minor side-effect as a major achievement of women's struggle for liberation. Presenting these cigarettes as a symbol of emancipation, and hence as the natural choice for the woman who thinks of herself as liberated, it builds an enclosure around the feminist movement, curtailing its more radical perspective.

In its alleged positive attitude to female emancipation this series of adverts is similar to an advert for a life insurance company offering a 'Women's Individual Savings Plan' (*Cosmopolitan*, July 1977).

This advert clearly adapts its sales strategies in order to capture the liberated women's market, for instance by borrowing from the Women's Lib register: 'designed by women, solely for women, with only the interests of women in mind'. In this way a ordinary insurance company is presenting itself as the avant-garde of female liberation, helping women to consolidate their new independent position.

The advert for Elizabeth Arden Cabriole fragrances uses a more reproachful, annoyed tone of voice (plate 39), the headline asking 'Why can't woman be like a woman?' The first paragraph of the body copy shows that this question is probably asked by a man, which may turn it into a warning: men think that Women's Lib has gone far enough; a beautiful woman is not necessarily an attractive woman, at least not if 'she thinks like a man, she acts like a man. Why can't she be more of a woman?'

In order to ask these two questions the source behind them must think he has access to the true meaning of femininity: why can't a person who is biologically a woman conform to the accepted social norms of female behaviour? Probably very few people think that women should achieve equality by imitating male behaviour. And probably even less people would dare to lay down the rules of a new, liberated female identity. Nevertheless, this is the project undertaken by this advert, whose solution is quite simple: liberation and equality belong in the sphere of work, but in the private sphere nothing basic has changed, so you are able to 'get the best of both worlds. To be feminist and feminine', which two concepts are neatly explained in a series of syntactic parallels:

feminist	*feminine*
gets the job, ability	fluttering her eyelashes
share the bill at lunch	not at dinner
a new confidence	waits for him to open the door
make decisions	let others think they've made them [decisions]

When this type of woman needs a fragrance, as women have for ages, her natural choice is Cabriole, a fragrance 'full of delicious contradictions. Exactly like the woman who's clever enough to enjoy being a woman.' This advert therefore addresses women engaged in a sometimes painful historical struggle for a new identity by assuring them that this struggle is compatible with a traditional female identity placed beyond history.

Why can't a woman be like a woman?

A man was explaining why he didn't find a particularly beautiful young woman attractive. "Because she thinks like a man, she acts like a man. Why can't she be more of a woman?"

In fact, there's never been a more rewarding time to be a woman. To get the best of both worlds. To be feminist and feminine.

Today's woman gets the job because of her ability and not by fluttering her eyelashes. She'll share the bill at lunch, but not at dinner.

She has a new confidence. But she waits for him to open the door.

She can make decisions. But she knows when to let others think they've made them.

Elizabeth Arden has a fragrance for today's woman. It's called Cabriole. It's not meant to change her life, rather it's meant to become part of it. It's for her private moments as well as her public moments. It's for the woman she is.

Cabriole Eau de Toilette and Parfum de Toilette.

Cabriole is full of delicious contradictions. Exactly like the woman who's clever enough to enjoy being a woman.

Elizabeth Arden

Dedicated to your beauty.

Plate 39   Cabriole
Cosmopolitan *July 1978*

The Londun Line hair straightener advert dealt with above (pp. 143-5, plate 36) cynically exploits the Black Power slogan 'Black is beautiful' to insult a Black identity, principally by making use of the ambiguity of 'Black' (Negro) vs. 'black' (colour).

In order to be black it is not sufficient to have black hair and skin; a Black identity comprises other features, for instance curly hair. The Londun Line advert pretends that 'Black' and 'black' are identical, which makes black hair sufficient justification for joining the 'Black is beautiful' slogan; this trick expands the number of potential buyers since it is supposedly not incompatible with a Black identity to have straight hair. This enables the advertiser to pervert the slogan by unblushingly putting the effect of his product in initial position: 'Straight, Black and Beautiful'.

This advert demonstrates how an advertiser who is bold enough to mention the main objection to his product (Black identity and pride) can effectively neutralize this objection, reducing it to a harmless commercial tool.

Recuperating from criticism of advertising

You see the advertisements with these marvellous looking models looking terribly slinky and with marvellous skins and you think, Oh I'll be like that in a week, so you rush out and buy it and you don't realise they're under three inches of make-up. (plate 21)

This advert, and numerous others like it, testifies to a widespread distrust of advertising among the public, a belief that adverts deceive us into buying by making exaggerated claims and giving misleading illustrations. It also demonstrates that individual adverts can turn this distrust of the advertising institution to their own advantage by appearing to take the consumer's side against the misinformation of other adverts.

The advert takes for granted the consumers' attitude that adverts are unreliable, but merely *refers* to this attitude in a manner which is designed to validate this particular advert by exempting it from the aura of unreliability. Advertising's attempts to make itself immune to criticism usually take this form of seriously reproaching other adverts for being false. More rarely, adverts parody other ones by using their structure or content, turning it upside-down, but few with such elegance and wit as Smirnoff (plate 40).

This example presupposes a familiarity with the medium of advertising and even with previous Smirnoff campaigns, for its effectiveness depends on such audience knowledge. Earlier, Smirnoff ran a series of adverts which pictured the amazing effects resulting from the consumption of Smirnoff vodka. These adverts were legally banned because of their excessive claims; one of them promised to be able to transport people from a low menial status to the jet set: 'I was Mr Holmes of Household Linens until I discovered Smirnoff. . . The effect is shattering' (cited by Williamson 1978: 176).

The present advert and the others in the series exploit the earlier ones by making hyperexaggerated claims for the product, claims which are so improbable that people will laugh at them — and remember them for their ingenuity in circumventing the ban *and* exploiting it for their own purposes. At the same time the reader gets the pleasure of working out a solution to the joke: this woman was a passenger of the Titanic when she ordered a Smirnoff cocktail which produced the 'shattering effect' (cf. the previous adverts) of sinking the *Titanic*. So the woman now finds herself in the water regretting that she didn't believe the Smirnoff people when 'they said anything could happen' — but supposedly convinced of its magic powers. (According to Mower (1981) this Smirnoff advert was banned by the Advertising Standards Authority which considered it deeply offensive to the relatives of those who had died on the *Titanic*.)

REFORMING ADVERTISING?

Faced with examples like the one just analysed, many scholars and critics are led to a very pessimistic appraisal of the possibilities of regulating advertising:

Advertisements (ideologies) can incorporate anything, even re-absorb criticism of themselves, because they refer to it, devoid of content. The whole system of advertising is a great recuperator: it will work on any material at all, it will bounce back uninjured from both advertising restriction laws and criticisms of its basic function

(Williamson 1978: 167).

Plate 40   Smirnoff
Mayfair *August 1977*

While agreeing with this appraisal of the system of advertising, we want to adduce the only advert in our smaple which seems to be an exception to the general rule; this example shows an advert which does not simply react to consumer criticism with recuperation, but which adapts to such criticism in a way which really serves consumer interests.

Through the display of the shampoos of unidentified competitors, combined with a humorous title of an old classic and a critical follow-up in the body copy, the Johnsons baby shampoo advert (plate 41) makes it clear that it takes the consumers' side against the ridiculous 'natural wild ingredients' of soaps and beauty potions: focus returns to the material use-value after a long excursion into the more exotic realms of herbs and fruit.

This advert categorizes all extracts of apple, wheatgerm, and so on as 'strange additives', 'weird ingredients' and the like, and straightforwardly dismisses brands offering different varieties for dry, normal, greasy and fly-away hair by saying that varying the dosage of one type will give the same effect.

On the one hand, therefore, this advert demonstrates that advertising is no static ideological phenomenon: it flexibly accommodates its messages to suit the changing climate of opinion among the consumers. Faced with a growing awareness and criticism of pollution, the people behind this advert are sensitive enough to realize that for some consumers 'additives', even supposedly 'natural ones', are changing from being a 'purr word' to a 'snarl word'. Consequently, they try to carve out for themselves a niche in the market where persuasion follows different lines from the rest of the market. Whether it remains a niche, or whether the niche may function as a bridgehead for raids into the surrounding territory will mainly be decided by factors external to advertising.

On the other hand, in spite of its honesty, this advert *is* an advert whose principal aim is to get us to buy. If we don't want to be caught off guard, we should be just as critical of this one as we are of less honest ones: being so scornful of the additives of other shampoos, why does Johnsons not tell us exactly what its ingredients are?

What this advert and the preceding ones (Cabriole, Londun Line, Smirnoff) show is that advertising is suceptible to real change; they also show unmistakably, however, that there are limits to the extent of such change. Whereas advertising can fairly easily accommodate

Yes, we have no bananas.

Nor do we go in for any other strange additives.

There's no room for them in a shampoo as pure and gentle as JOHNSON'S Baby Shampoo.

It cleans your hair gently without harshly stripping off all the essential oils or leaving any strange ones behind. So all the health and beauty of your hair shines through.

If it's normal for your hair to be a bit greasy, use a little more shampoo. If it's on the dry side, use less.

Of course there will always be people who will be tempted by shampoos with weird ingredients.

But for those who agree that additives are best left out, there's JOHNSON'S Baby Shampoo.

The one that won't drive your hair bananas.

The purest, gentlest shampoo money can buy.

Plate 41   Johnson's Baby Shampoo
Cosmopolitan *July 1977*

consumer criticism of certain raw materials — which requires nothing but the exchange of one ingredient for another — it is impossible for it to accommodate to social and political criticism without endangering the whole foundation of the social order on which capitalism and advertising depend. In the latter case, advertising has to apply its recuperative capacities in order to neutralize the criticism.

The American *Ms Magazine* features a page called 'One Step Forward', which pictures a selection of positive advertising images 'that prove change possible — and keep optimism alive' (editorial comment, April 1981). In the same issue 'One Step Forward' salutes adverts 'that recognize the career potential of both boys and girls', for instance one picturing a two-year old girl accompanied by the sentence: 'The future President of the United States deserves a nice dry place to grow up in. And there's no drier diaper than Quilted Pampers.' In other issues the feature has shown a father pushing a pram, genuine uncompetitive female relationships, and so on.

Such adverts, in our opinion, are to be preferred to the majority of today's advertising images, but those who wish to see merely an increased amount of 'positive adverts' seem to forget a basic feature of advertising: its effects are not only a consequence of its misrepresentation of, say, female and male roles, but in the first place a consequence of its misrepresentation of *human* relationships and feelings, which are made dependent on purchased commodities. By tying our relationships and feelings to commodities, adverts set the bounds of such relationships and feelings and detract from our spontaneity. Because of its fascinating images there is a tendency for advertising to transform all human reactions into predetermined, self-conscious poses.

This concern about the colourful images of advertising is shared by Williamson (1978: 175) who is worried not only because of their function as models of behaviour, but because of their persuasive mechanisms, and she is very pessimistic about any attempt to reform advertising:

You may not really believe that some minor ingredient is going to transform your casserole into a cordon-bleu dish, but the *images* of the grateful, hungry, appreciative husband and son tucking into a hearty meal provided by the woman, stay long after the actual claims made on behalf of the product have been forgotten. . . whatever restrictions are made in

Plate 42   Hoover
Woman *October 1977*

terms of their verbal content or 'false claims', there is no way of getting at their use of images and symbols.

Unless you want to follow a proposal from a research report on the portrayal of sex roles in advertising, commissioned by the Danish Consumer Ombudsman, suggesting that all portrayals of human beings in ads should be banned.

The benefits of implementing this proposal and removing people from ads can be illustrated by a Hoover advert (plate 42). As it appears on the page, the kitchen utensils are connected with a woman's face through her relayed (cf. pp. 35-6) message that we should 'insist on Hoover for good looks and reliability'. Without the small inset photo we would avoid the absurd ambiguity of the 'good looks' and be left with a fairly sober advert with big clear pictures of the commodities, supplemented by useful bits of information — which might of course be increased for the achievement of optimal consumer information.

However, we may propose various restrictions on the visual and verbal parts of adverts separately, and still not be certain to achieve our objective of avoiding the individualized collective deceit of advertising.

With or without reforms and restrictions, advertising remains a commercial institution whose ideological messages reach far beyond a mere commercial impact, always ready to offer 'a neat solution for the man who wants to live at peace with his weaknesses', helping him to 'substantiate even the most elaborate deceit' (Amplex Breath Freshener, *Mayfair*, August 1977).

Notes

1 ADVERTISING AND SOCIETY

1 In 1975 the average proportion of advertising revenue of British national newspapers in relation to total revenue was about 30 per cent for populars and 60 per cent for qualities. Source: Royal Commission on the Press, 1976.
2 The principles of the sphere of circulation are described in Marx's *Capital*, vol. I parts I-II; for an introduction to Marxist economy, see e.g. Mandel (1970) or McLelland (1975).
3 In 1973 press advertising accounted for 71 per cent of total advertising expenditure and TV advertising for 24 percent. These percentages have remained relatively constant since 1960. Source: *Advertising Quarterly*, 40, 1974.
4. In 1971 42 per cent of married women in Britain were employed outside the home (source: *Women and Work*, 1974).

2 LANGUAGE AND COMMUNICATION

1 This observation is originally Jakobson's (1960). In recent years it has been developed in various ways by various writers; see Criper and Widdowson (1975: 195-200), Halliday (1973: 9-21), Leech (1974: 47-50).
2 See the British Code of Advertising Practice, which is based on the International Code of Advertising Practice, and is operated by the Advertising Standards Authority (ASA), 15-17 Ridgmount Street, London WC1E 7AW.
3 See especially pp. 172-91. For critical introductory discussions in English, see Scholes (1974: 102-11) and Culler (1975: 75-95).
4 Classical rhetoric actually draws a distinction between metonymy, which is a relationship of contiguity (e.g. 'Whitehall' for 'the British

Government') and synechdoche, which is a part/whole relationship (e.g. 'the crown' for 'the king'). Following Jakobson (1956: 90 ff.) we collapse them into one, since both figures rest on the indexical relationship.
5 The idea that the denotation of an image is not culturally coded has been seriously questioned by Eco (1976: 191).

3   THE STRUCTURE OF AN ADVERTISEMENT

1 Incidently, in the material studied, this advert appeared only in *Woman* and *She,* which are mainly read by married women (cf. above pp. 11-12), but not in *Cosmopolitan.*

4   STRATEGIES OF ADDRESS: SEX AND CLASS

1 Or in Barthes's (1967: 41) term: the product is semanticized; cf. above p. 6-7.
2 Originally proposed by F. Parkin, *Class Inequality and Political Order* (London: Paladin, 1972), these meaning systems are discussed in Hall (1973).
3 Unfortunately, we have not been able to obtain permission to reproduce the advert referred to.

5   ADVERTISING AS A PYSCHOLOGICAL MIRROR

1 The social pattern which we have outlined here seems to have been prevalent in traditional working-class and rural communities (cf. Frankenberg, 1966; Young and Willmott, 1962). To a certain extent it still survives in some marginal working-class communities (cf. Milroy, 1980).
2 Unfortunately, we have not been able to obtain permission to reproduce the advert referred to.

6   THE IDEOLOGY OF ADVERTISING

1 This definition of ideology is influenced mainly by Althusserian ideological theory. For a theoretical introduction the reader is referred to Hall (1977), which includes a bibliography of primary theoretical works.

2 See Hall (1977: 323-5).

3 As will be evident, we are greatly indebted to Judith Williamson's *Decoding Advertisements* (1978) in the following sections.

4 Such an object or person with a known value is called 'objective correlative' by Judith Williamson, borrowing T. S. Eliot's term from aesthetic theory:

> The only way to express an emotion in the form of art is by finding an 'objective correlative': in other words, *a set of objects*, situation, a chain of events, which shall be the formula of that particular emotion; such that when external facts, which must terminate in sensory experience, are given, the emotion is immediately evoked.
>
> (T. S. Eliot, 'Hamlet', in *Selected Essays*, Faber and Faber, 1932, p. 145)

Bibliography

Anderson, J. M. 1977. *On Case Grammar*. London: Croom Helm.

Barthes R. 1964. Rhétorique de l'image. *Communications* 4, 40-51. (English translation: Rhetoric of the image. In R. Barthes, *Image music text*. London: Fontana/Collins, 1977, 32-51.)

—— 1967. *Elements of Semiology*. London: Cape.

Berger, J. 1972. *Ways of Seeing*. Harmondsworth: Penguin Books and BBC.

British Press, The, 1976. London: Her Majesty's Stationery Office.

Brown, J. A. C. 1963. *Techniques of Persuasion*. Harmondsworth: Penguin.

Criper, C. and Widdowson, H. G. 1975. Sociolinguistics and language teaching. In J. P. B. Allen and S. P. Corder, *Papers in Applied Linguistics*. London: Oxford University Press, 155-217.

Culler, J. 1975. *Structuralist Poetics: Structuralism, linguistics and the Study of Literature*. London: Routledge & Kegan Paul.

Curran, J., Gurevitch, M. and Woollacott, J. (eds), 1977. *Mass Communication and Society*. Edward Arnold and the Open University.

Eco, U. 1972. *Einführung in die Semiotik*. München: Wilhelm Fink. (Italian original: *La struttura assente*. Milan 1968.)

—— 1976. *A Theory of Semiotics*. Bloomington and London: Indiana University Press.

Faulder, C. 1977. Advertising. In J. Kind and M. Stott (eds), *Is this your Life? Images of Women in the Media*. London: Virago, 37-64.

Fillmore, C. J. 1968. The case for case. In E. Bach and R. T. Harms (eds), *Universals in Linguistic Theory*. New York: Holt, 1-88.

—— 1971. Some problems for case grammar. *Working Papers in Linguistics* 10, pp. 245-65. Ohio State University.

Fiske, J. and Hartley J. 1978. *Reading television*. London: Methuen.

Frankenberg, R. 1966. *Communities in Britain*. Harmondsworth: Pelican.

Goffman, E. 1979. *Gender Advertisements*. London: Macmillan.

Gombrich, E. H. 1963. *Meditations on a Hobby Horse*. London: Phaidon Press.

Greimas, A. J. 1966. *Sémantique structurale*. Paris: Larousse.

Hall, S. 1973. Encoding and ecoding in the television discourse. Centre for Contemporary Cultural Studies, Birmingham, *Occasional Papers*, no. 7.

—— 1977. Culture, media and 'the ideological effect'. In Curran *et al.*, 315-48.

Halliday, M. A. K. 1967. Notes on transitivity and theme in English, part 2. *Journal of Linguistics* 3, 199-244.

—— 1970. Language structure and language function. In J. Lyons (ed.) *New Horizons in Linguistics*. Harmondsworth: Penguin, 140-65.

—— 1973. *Explorations in the Functions of Language*. London: Edward Arnold.

Halliday, M. A. K. and Hasan, R. 1976. *Cohesion in English*. London: Longman.

Harris, R. and Seldon A. 1962. *Advertising and the Public*. London: André Deutsch.

Haug, W. F. 1971. *Kritik der Warenästhetik*. Frankfurt am Main: Suhrkamp.

Huddleston, R. D. 1971. *The Sentence in Written English*. Cambridge: Cambridge University Press.

Jakobson, R. 1956. Two aspects of language and two types of aphasic disturbances. In R. Jakobson and M. Halle, *Fundamentals of Language*. The Hague: Mouton, 69-96.

—— 1960. Linguistics and poetics. In T. A. Sebeok (ed.), *Style and Language*. Cambridge, Mass.: MIT Press, 350-77. Reprinted in J. P. B. Allen and S. P. Corder (eds), *Readings for Applied Linguistics*. London: Oxford University Press, 1973, 53-7.

Jones, B. 1982a. How we grew along with you. *Cosmopolitan*, March 1982.

—— 1982b. Portrait of you now: *Cosmopolitan* survey results. *Cosmopolitan*, March 1982.

Key, W. B. 1973. *Subliminal Seduction*. New York: Signet.

Klein, V. 1965. *Britain's Married Woman Workers*. London: Routledge & Kegan Paul.

Leech, G. N. 1966. *English in Advertising*. London: Longman.

—— 1969. *A Linguistic Guide to English Poetry*. London: Longman.

—— 1971. *Meaning and the English Verb*. London: Longman.

—— 1974. *Semantics*. Harmondsworth: Penguin.

Lund, J. V. 1947. *Newspaper Advertising*. New York: Prentice-Hall.

Lyons, J. 1977. *Semantics 1-2*. Cambridge: Cambridge University Press.

Mandel, E. 1970. *An Introduction to Marxist Economic Theory*. New York: Pathfinder Press.

Marx, K. 1887. *Capital*, vol. I. Moscow: Progress Publishers.

McLelland, D. 1975. *Marx*. Glasgow: Fontana/Collins.

Millum, T. 1975. *Images of Woman. Advertising in Women's Magazines*. London: Chatto & Windus.

Milroy, L. 1980. *Language and Social Networks*. Oxford: Blackwell.

Mower, S. 1981. Would you buy shoes from advertising like this? *Cosmopolitan*, October 1981.

National Readership Survey, 1976-7. Joint Industry Committee for National Readership Surveys (JICNRS).

Norins, H. 1966. *The Compleat Copywriter*. New York: McGraw-Hill.

Packard, V. 1957. *The Hidden Persuaders*. Harmondsworth: Penguin.

Peirce, C. S. 1960. *Collected Papers of Charles Sanders Peirce* ed. by C. Hartshorne and P. Weiss, vol. 2: *Elements of Logic*. Cambridge, Mass.: Harvard University Press.

Reekie, W. G. 1974. *Advertising. Its Place in Political and Managerial Economics*. London: Macmillan.

Rommetveit, R. 1968. *Words, Meanings, and Messages*. New York and London: Academic Press.

Royal Commission on The Press 1976. *The National Newspaper industry*. London: Her Majesty's Stationery Office.

Rysman, A. 1977. How the gossip became woman. *Journal of Communication*, winter 1977.

Scholes, R. 1974. *Structuralism in Literature. An Introduction*. New Haven and London: Yale University Press.

Searle, J. R. 1969. *Speech Acts*. London: Cambridge University Press.

—— 1971. What is a speech act? In J. R. Searle (ed.), *The Philosophy of Language*. London: Oxford University Press.

Stevens, P. 1972. *I Can Sell You Anything*. New York: Peter Wyden.

Turner, E. S. 1965. *The Shocking History of Advertising*. Harmondsworth: Penguin.

White, C. 1970. *Women's Magazines*. London: Michael Joseph.

Widdowson, H. G. 1973. Directions in the Teaching of discourse. In S. P. Corder and E. Roulet (eds), *Theoretical Linguistic Models in Applied Linguistics*. Brussels/Paris: AIMAV/Didier.

—— 1978. *Teaching Language as Communication*. Oxford: Oxford University Press.

Wight, R. 1972. *The Day the Pigs Refused to be Driven to the Market*. London: Hart-Davis, MacGibbon.

Williamson, J. 1978. *Decoding Advertisements. Ideology and meaning in Advertising*. London: Marion Boyars.

Winship, J. 1980. Sexuality for sale. In S. Hall, D. Hobson, A. Lowe and P. Willis (eds), *Culture, Media, Language*. London: Hutchinson, 217-23.

Women and Work 1974. London: HMSO.

Young, M. and Willmott, P. 1962. *Family and Kinship in East London*. Harmondsworth: Penguin.

Index

Actants, 27-9, 94
advertising
    and capitalism, 7-9, 146-7, 155
    cultural function of, 139-40
    regulation of, 5, 103-4, 168-74
    as a social ritual, 120-2
    types of, 1-3, 150
aestheticization of commodities
        (*Warenästhetik*), 8-9, 65, 78, 154-5
    as ideologization, 155
anchorage/relay, 34-6, 52, 56, 100, 102
Anderson, J. M., 29
attention catchers, 58-66

Barthes, R., 5, 34-5, 42, 73, 176
behavioural normalcy, 141-5
Berger, J., 81, 82, 87, 110, 115, 118, 148
Brown, J. A. C., 10

capitalism, 7-8
    distrust of, 131-3, 147
case grammar, 29-32
clichés, 80, 84
cohesion and coherence, 18-20, 57
commodity profiles, 74-5
connotation/denotation, 42-4, 79
credibility, 66, 117-18
Criper, C., 16, 175
Culler, J., 27, 175

day-dreams, 117-18, 122
deictic/deixis, 17, 34
domesticity, 79-81

Eco, U., 36, 43, 50, 176
entailment, 24
expectation, 24-7, 58, 121, 129, 143

Faulder, C., 80
femininity, images of, 75, 79-106, 142,
        165
    the beauty ideal, 81-7
    deceit, 84
    domesticity, 79-81
    and envy, 87
    and independence, 88-90, 164-5
    multiple identity, 100-2
    servant, 103
    and solidarity, 93-9
    whore, 102-3
Fillmore, C. J., 29
Fiske, J., 111, 113, 121
Frankenberg, R., 126, 176
gender identities, 73-4, 108-9
    female, 75, 79-106
    male, 75-9, 90-3, 102-7
Goffman, E., 100, 102
Gombrich, E. H., 36
gossip, 82, 93-9
Greimas, A. J., 27

Hall, S., 110, 145, 147, 149, 152, 176-7
Halliday, M. A. K., 16, 19, 21, 175
Harris, J., 111, 113, 121
Hartley, J., 111, 113, 121
Hasan, R., 19
Haug, W. F., 8-9, 155
Huddleston, R. D., 57
hyperbolic claims, 58-60

icon, 36, 39
ideology, 121, 124, 145-6, 147, 152
implicit content, 23-7
index, 38-9
individualization, 61, 111-12, 140, 148-9
information structure, 21-3

Jakobson, R., 16, 175
Jones, B., 88-90

Key, W. B., 103

language functions, 16-17, 52-4, 56-7,
    67-70
Leech, G. N., 1, 9, 15, 16, 22, 24, 35,
    44, 52, 57, 62, 175
Lund, J. V., 46, 49
Lyons, J., 34

McLelland, D., 7, 175
Mandel, E., 7, 175
market consciousness, 146-8
masculinity, images of, 75-9, 90-3, 102-8
    family father, 90
    the 'new man', 90-3
    sexual animal, 104-6
    success image, 106
Marx, K., 7, 175
meaning transfer, 152-6, 162
metaphor, 38, 41-2, 52, 57, 62, 153
metonymy, 38, 106, 153
Millum, T., 12
Milroy, L., 126, 176
mirror technique, 84
Mower, S., 89, 103, 168
multiple identity, 100-2

Nature/natural, 156-61
needs, material and social, 5-6, 10, 60,
    73, 75

Norins, H., 13
norm-transcending adverts, 135

Packard, V., 5
participant roles, 27-32
Peirce, C. S., 36
presupposition, 24-6, 154
problem-perceptive adverts, 135, 139-40
problem reduction, 142-5

readership, 10-12
Reekie, W. G., 5-6, 9
referent systems, 152, 155-63
    assimilation of, 163-8
relay, *see* anchorage
Rommetveit, R., 17
Rysman, A., 93

Scholes, R., 27, 175
Searle, J. R., 16
social class, 10-12, 61, 110-16, 149-52,
    163
social networks, 126-7
Stevens, P., 26
subliminal seduction, 103
symbol, 36-42

Turner, E. S., 4

use value, 8-9, 78

Warenästhetik, *see* aestheticization
Widdowson, H. G., 16, 19, 175
Wight, R., 2, 26
Williamson, J., 80, 100, 127,
    149, 152, 153, 155, 157-8, 160,
    164, 168, 172, 177
Willmott, P., 126, 176
Winship, J., 74

Young, M., 126, 176